PLANET IDIOT
A Survival Guide

by Lindsey Stokes

"I can't tell you how much I enjoyed *Planet Idiot*! Read it! Lindsey Stokes is a funny lady, if I do say so myself."

Garrison Keillor, **author**

"I'm not worthy. Quick-witted columnist Lindsey Stokes refers to the large self-help section in bookstores and questions, 'Is it just me, or does Deepak Chopra, guru to everything, look like some sort of mental patient?' Such comical barbs catch you off guard throughout her new book, and she'll have you rolling on the floor. Stokes takes life's problems and puts them in perspective, forcing us to let loose and laugh at ourselves."

Angela Cortez, **Denver Post**

"Lindsey Stokes' unique observations on the human condition are sharp, funny and unpredictable. She's absolutely destined to become one of America's favorite writers."

Los Angeles Business Journal

"Lindsey Stokes is terrific! *Planet Idiot* is a fun, funny, unstintingly unserious jab at the seriousness all around us. Anyone who can stick a pin in the rump of the pompous civic leader, the manic Federal Express driver, the phony wine connoisseur, and Nietzsche, all without being mean, is okay by me! I laughed a lot!"

Paul Vitello, **Newsday**

"Where did this lady come from, this Lindsey Stokes who is writing the very same thoughts that I'm thinking as some numb-nuts cuts me off on the freeway, only with better metaphors and sharper words?! If she were working in the next cubicle, I would consider taking early retirement and starting each day with her over morning coffee."

Jon Hahn, **Seattle Post-Intelligencer**

Planet Idiot

Planet Idiot

A Survival Guide

❧

Lindsey Stokes

GREENWICH PRESS • 2001

Published by
Greenwich Press
4412 Spicewood Springs Road, Suite 102
Austin, Texas 78759

Library of Congress Cataloging-in-Publication Data

Stokes, Lindsey.
　Planet Idiot : a survival guide / by Lindsey Stokes
　-- 1st ed.
　p.　cm.
　ISBN 0-9705061-0-4

　1. American wit and humor.　I. Title.

PN6162.S76 2001　　　　　818'.6
　　　　　　　　　　　　QBI00-901988

Designed by Henry Hutchins

Printed in the United States of America

First Edition

For John,
Jack and Skyler

To the moon and back . . .

Acknowledgments

Lucky me. In addition to being surrounded by Idiots, I just so happen to know several exceptions to the rule.

Jim Hornfischer, my literary agent, is one of them. I thank him first, and foremost, for sticking with me. I also thank him for his brilliant, diplomatic editing, and for all of his terrific ideas. He brought an incredible amount of knowledge, direction, enthusiasm, and spark to this book.

Paul Williams, my newspaper agent, has been with me, tirelessly, from the very beginning. I thank him for driving newspaper editors around the country crazy, so that I wouldn't have to, and for cutting a path.

Leann, Gus, Marika, and Andy at Phenix & Phenix brought an amazing, high-energy, and no-nonsense push to this book that, from early on, had my head spinning. I'm so grateful for their drive and commitment.

Thanks, also, to my "creative advisors" and research staff, including Jack Sprat, Skyrocket, Cecelia, Mutton, Leigh-Leigh Belle, and Timmo.

This book wouldn't have been possible without three very special people.

My dad, who has never been very impressed with even the toughest of challenges, obstacles, or setbacks, has managed, somehow, to pass a fraction of his strength, spirit, and resilience on to me. I thank him, with whole heart, for leading by example.

My mom, Poster Woman for passion and enthusiasm, fuels me, both personally and professionally, with an infinite bunker of high-octane support and appreciation. I thank her, with whole heart, for always being right there next to me, holding my hand, even when she's not.

Finally, I thank "Mr. Wonderful," who has, day after day, year after year, completely redefined the word "supportive." I thank him for taking on this book project in the same manner in which he takes on most things—with a quiet, but unrelenting, determination. Thanks, John, for somehow managing to make this—and so many other things—possible.

Lucky me.

Contents

Part IV—Look on the Bright Side

Part V—Uh, Priorities, Anyone?

Part VI—The World Is Full of Idiots

A Final Word

"Beyond its entertainment value, Baywatch *has enriched and, in many cases, helped save lives. I'm looking forward to the opportunity to continue with a project which has had such significance for so many."*
—Actor David Hasselhoff

ℬ

"It takes all kinds, Linds."
—B. R. Stokes

FOREWORD

Planet Idiot

There's so much inherent pain and suffering in life—disease, death, drug abuse, hunger, homelessness, reality-based TV, plans for a new Britney Spears museum—it strikes me, frankly, that we certainly don't need to create more.

Nonetheless, most of us live our lives like TV newscasters: we hype and exaggerate the bad stuff, padding the rest of our air time with meaningless banter. Jaws clenched, veins popping out of our foreheads, we scurry through our days, our lives, with a sense of urgency that ought to be limited to situations in which Klingon vessels have us locked on target and (damn it, Scottie!) the shields are down.

And what's more, we're consumed, *competitive even*, about our complex problems, convinced that our lives are busier and more demanding than everyone else's.

"I'm busy."

"Me, too. I'm really busy."

"I'm going nuts, I'm so unbelievably, incredibly busy."

"I'm so busy, I had breakfast last night."

"I don't have time for breakfast! I've got an I.V. line running straight into my arm. Also, since I don't have time to go to the bathroom, I have a catheter."

It's weird.

Oh sure, not as weird, perhaps, as the Teamsters local in Oakland, California, which protested Mills College's use of goats to clear brush on its land, suggesting that the college ought to either replace the goats with its members, or "unionize the goats." But still. Weird.

In an effort to combat these ongoing woe-is-me, idiotic melodramatics, we've started a new tradition at my house. Something we should've started a long time ago. At dinnertime we proceed around the table, each of us naming at least one thing that was terrific about the day.

It's a refreshing exercise. Particularly when you consider the fact that my young son often offers up such grateful revelations as, "One thing that was really good about my day is that I didn't stick peas, or rocks, or anything up my nose."

Great. Double bonus. Not having to do nostril excavations with the sort of medical tools normally found in the silverware drawer is a real highlight of my day, too.

Nasal passageways not withstanding, learning to focus on the positive, take stock of what's right, *and actively appreciate it*, as opposed to staggering around in all the negative crud, takes practice. Particularly since, at every stage in life, in every situation—we are surrounded by idiots.

Idiots who are destined to go through Life so focused on the "static," that they can't hear the *music*. So focused on the static, that they can't hear the *traffic and weather*. So focused on the static, that they can't hear the *news at the top of the hour*. So focused on this metaphor that it may be time to sign up for an obscure literary workshop in the backwoods of New Hampshire.

Idiots make it their life's work to impress others. They never understand what is really important in life. They breed with other idiots, creating all sorts of miniature, little idiots. The Little Idiots eventually become the Big Pillar Idiots of our society—inept bosses, Nazi homeowners' associations, clueless spouses, unruly children, moron drivers, and the sort of restaurant waiters who insist on smothering your sandwich with expensive Dijon mustard when you *specifically requested* the cheap stuff.

They're everywhere.

The last time I went to New York, I arrived from the west coast on a red-eye. I showed up at the hotel where I'd pre-paid my non-refundable reservation with a credit card. It was raining and I was pregnant.

"Sorry, we gave your room away when you didn't show up," the woman at the front desk informed me. "And we're totally booked."

"I paid for that room, it was mine until check-out."

"But you weren't here."

"I'm here now. That's my room until check-out."

"We assumed you weren't coming."

"I PAID IN ADVANCE FOR THAT ROOM!"

"There's nothing I can do," she said. And I believed her. Do you know why? Do you?! BECAUSE SHE WAS AN IDIOT! She'd gone to Advanced Idiocy school. She majored in Pretension and Attitude. She spent summers at Camp Butthead.

The same camp my local Federal Express delivery guy went to. I mean, does he really need to get out of his truck at my house swinging a bat? Waving a can of mace? Hissing, growling, and making murderous death threats to my dogs? I feel it sends a bad message. The body language is all off.

So when my dogs react to the baiting, running him down like a hapless wildebeast on the sub-Saharan plain, and when a hotel employee looks at an exhausted, drenched, pregnant woman and says, "there are no rooms at the inn," I try to look for a lesson in all this.

Namely, we live on Planet Idiot.

A-ha! you say. You've found your own life filled with idiots. Starbucks idiots who fill your cup halfway, when you've specifically stated, "No, I don't need any room for cream." Parent idiots who don't quite get the fact that their kids are pains-in-the-rear, smiling bemusedly as their little darlings chase the neighbors' cats. Career-driven idiots who look constipated, on and off the job.

What can a non-idiot possibly do to remain functional amidst all this idiocy? You're expecting to get that right here? *In the blasted introduction?* What are you, an idiot?

Oh sure, I could tell you what's important in my life—a disconnected answering machine, a house bigger than Aaron Spelling's, a dream that, someday, all soups would be chunky enough that we could eat them with a fork, a hope that my bank teller will stop making me show I.D. when I'm *depositing cash*, for the love of God—but that wouldn't necessarily be your version.

In a nutshell, this book is a compass. A road map. A survival guide. It will teach you, my friend, how to navigate your way through all the Idiots and Their Workings, how to focus on priorities, and how to laugh in the face of fear, challenges, pain, and your partner's sexual performance. I will present real-life situations to you, situations within which we all find ourselves, and I will offer specific, usable, advice. Lessons. Tidbits to email to your friends and family, or stick up on the fridge at work. Or to place under the short leg of the kitchen table.

Yes, in just a few minutes a day, you will learn how to be happy, successful, and at total peace in your life, while firming your thighs, making a fortune in the stock market, and planning an inexpensive, but imaginative, dinner party using empty toilet paper rolls for center pieces!

And in the end, you will have all the skills necessary for living among all the blasted turkey-butts, right here on beautiful Planet Idiot.

PART I

LEARN TO LAUGH

People often turn to me for advice. They say, "Lindsey, how can I be happy, fulfilled and entirely content with life—in less than three minutes a day while making a lot of money and firming my thighs—while I'm surrounded by idiots?"

I look back at them in a calm, all-knowing, Dalai Lama sort of way, touch my hand soothingly on their shoulders, and say, "Apparently, you haven't seen my thighs, lately."

Nonetheless, I have found an inner peace, a sense of quiet contentment about the harmony of life, despite the fact that the world is full of obnoxious, insecure, loud-mouthed *idiots* whom I'd like to *run over at full-speed with my four-wheel-drive sport-utility vehicle.*

Sorry.

Back to my inner peace and how I got it.

I started searching for inner peace when it occurred to me, a few years ago, that it was a saner alternative to, say, full-blown lunacy. Perhaps it was the fascist Homeowners' Association memorandum that stipulated the non-removal of poison oak because, and I quote, *"it looks beautiful in the fall."* I offered to put them all in drug rehab programs.

Perhaps it was the 946th time that my husband left gunked-up and mangled dental floss on the bathroom counter. Perhaps it was the crushing societal pressure, and my stalwart refusal, to call a "large" coffee at Starbucks a *"grande."*

But frankly, I suspect the life-transforming inner-harmony thing may have kicked in when my young son, who had shown an early, if not disturbing, interest in bodily functions, shouted, "Does *that* man go PEE-PEE?" pointing at an elderly gentleman in the grocery store. Who was all of six inches away. I took a deep, cleansing breath, I recall, smiled an incredibly fake smile at the fellow whose urine production was in question, then commented to my son in the psychotically controlled tone of voice normally associated with serial killers, "Yes, honey. Everybody, uh, urinates, honey."

"HUH?! You mean, he goes *PEE-PEE?"*

"Are you hungry, sweetie? Do you want some candy? Do you want some toys? How about some cigarettes? Ever had a Harvey Wallbanger?"

"In the POTTY SEAT? Or in his DIAPER?"

Life is full of special moments, isn't it? Fortunately, Bladder Man had, by this point, developed a vigorous interest in such check-out magazines as *Teen People* and a tabloid featuring an exclusive on Elizabeth Taylor having two heads.

To my credit, I stayed calm. I cracked my molars, but I stayed calm. I've gotten so good at maintaining this inner-peace, Yoda-mind-control thing that I can even cope with the fact that sometimes I get irate letters from people—and this is only a hunch—whose daily fiber intake is *way* too low.

"Dear Leslie," they'll write, indicating how closely they've read and studied my weekly newspaper columns, which typically include a little thing called a BY-LINE. "If I ever see you on the streets, I'm going to reach for your throat, maim you, and then leave you in the gutter for having the GALL to suggest in your recent column that 'summer is a nice time of year.' WHO IN GOD'S NAME DO YOU THINK YOU ARE? I'm a WINTER person! I like COLD weather! Isotoners are my life! Snow removal is my livelihood! You've insensitively attacked those of us who don't like UV lenses!"

Another time, when I wrote a column in which I allegedly accepted an Academy Award, a rollicking literary satire, if I may say so myself, I got a letter accusing me of being part of some massive CIA-like network.

Uh, hello? Does someone need a few days at the lake?

Finally, last summer, when I was at the local nursery buying lovely plants and flowers to replace all the ones I regularly kill, two customers waiting in line got into a thing.

"I was here first!"

"I was waiting before you!"

"Liar!"

"Oh yeah? Well, why don't you go soak your head, fatso?"

It was all so warm and fuzzy. And yet, despite all this, as I've said, I've found inner harmony. I've learned to laugh.

Of course, sometimes it's a semi-crazed, manic, highly unstable sort of laugh, one that bounces around between various octaves, the kind of outburst that trained criminologists might associate with someone right on the brink. And yes, I have little imaginary friends. And sometimes I hear voices. And the voices say, over and over, ". . . in the valley, of the jolly—HO HO HO—*Greeeen* Giant."

But still. I laugh.

We all have pressures in our lives. We all have problems. I mean, just take a look at the scads of titles in the self-help section of your local bookstore or library. Have you wondered about some of the authors? Is it just me, or does Deepak Chopra, guru to everything, look like some sort of mental patient?

And John Gray? Mr. *Men Are From Mars, Women Are From Venus*, and I'm From a Yet Un-named Planet. What's the deal with this guy? He's so obsessed with calling men "Martians" and women "Venutians" that I've heard he calls his own mailman the "Mail Martian."

And this whole *Chicken Soup* series? I was tempted to come up with my own installment, *Chicken Soup for the Car-Crazed: 101 Heart-Warming Stories about Road Rage*. I mean, hey, just because you want to kill someone with your automobile doesn't mean you don't have a need for warm, cuddly stories, too.

Apparently life is hard. A task of Sisyphean proportions! Bills and mortgage payments. Job stress, marital issues, the endless juggling of multiple roles and demands, strange and inappropriate facial hairs, the sudden onslaught of gingivitis.

But enough about me.

Let's try to put things in perspective, shall we? Let's count our blessings. There's so much out there in the world with which to fill our hearts.

For instance, Tony Orlando and Dawn are no longer recording. Also, you almost never see Fabio anymore. And in Singapore, pedestrians are often struck by televisions, flower pots, old bikes, toaster ovens, and whatever else high-rise apartment dwellers decide to get rid of by throwing out their windows.

So you have to learn to laugh! You have to. Even when your toddler is on the public address system talking about pee. Even when you offend the Snow Removal Association of America.

Even when you curl up in the fetal position and commune with your special friend, the Jolly Green Giant.

Because *what is the alternative*? People are idiots, life is idiotic. If you focus on the junk mail, you're going to miss your government check. And you're going to be approximately as calm and relaxed as the Riverdance cast.

1

Laugh at Your Insecurities

I was lurking in the shadows, scanning, performing a little reconnaissance mission as I worked the remains of a canape out of my teeth.

I used to hate going to parties; I hated making conversation. I felt awkward, unimportant, inadequate without a new diamond-studded dress designed personally for me by Ralphie Lauren, without a staff of writers to make me sound witty and intelligent. I wasn't born gracious and confident. So I dealt with these situations in a very adult and sophisticated way—I started to scratch feverishly at my scalp, as if I had major head lice.

But I got sick of acting that way, particularly since my head was starting to bleed. I decided to try a new track. Lurking there in the shadows, what with the onion dip all gone, I decided to try something different.

"*SO*," I said in a really loud voice, stepping up to a group of folks chatting animatedly, "Anyone here ever been to Duluth?"

Silence. They weren't taking my bait. Perhaps I'd misjudged their interest in geography. I flushed, regrouped, and took another shot.

"Anyone ever stick a Q-tip in too far? Is that a mother or what?" I offered.

One of the group members turned, squinted at me and said, "Excuse me, do we *know you?*"

It worked! I'd engaged them in conversation!

"I LOVE IT WHEN YOU JOKE LIKE THAT! YOU BIG, NUTTY KIDDER!" I said, slapping him on the back hard enough, I suspect, to alter his memory of third grade.

You see, it's as simple as that, my friends. Once you are able to laugh at your astonishing number of well-earned insecurities, the art of party-going, mingling, and making interesting conversation with total strangers becomes possible.

Initially, I was careful. I talked mostly about the room temperature. Later, I ventured into discussions related to the location of the bathroom. Eventually, I broke into edgier material, stuff like, "Oh, excuse me," when I bumped into someone.

Then there was talk of dip. "This dip is good. Do you like the dip? What kind of dip is this? Do you buy dip? How often?"

Oh sure, sometimes I'd start sweating. Sometimes I worried that my hair needed work. Sometimes I felt like an idiot. And then I realized what would help—to laugh! I'd laugh and have the world laugh with me!

I tried two approaches—the Subtle and the Direct. Both work well when one is feeling insecure.

The Subtle approach involves lurking around the perimeter of a group, like a starving hyena stalking zebras, occasionally moving in closer, perhaps even peeking over their shoulders to inquire about the partially eaten stuffed mushrooms lying on their plates.

"If you're like me, you hate to see good food go to waste!" I might offer, laughing heartily, while at the same time demonstrating my sensitivity to our planet's natural resources.

The Direct approach is more direct—hence its name—and calls for jumping right in.

"Is it just me, or does it *blow any of you people away* that the Rothschilds had such *spectacular success* in governmental finance in the nineteenth century?" and then I'd burst out laughing. Who, for God's sake, doesn't laugh themselves silly just thinking about those nutty Rothschilds?

In more casual settings, another technique I frequently use is: "Okay, show of hands: *How many of you like to pull your Oreos apart and eat the filling first?*" You can kick-start the hilarity by eating a couple of actual Oreos prior to asking the question, then smiling at your target audience with chocolate smeared all over your teeth. Or, my other favorite line is: *"Excuse me, has anyone seen my cat?"* People love to help out when it comes to small, domesticated animals. Then, when I tell them that I don't even have a cat, if they aren't really pissed off, or anything, they have a good laugh.

Boom, now you're in. Stay with it, babe. You've done the hard part. Sustain the banter.

One way to keep a conversation lively when I'm feeling nervous about what to say next, is to periodically slap the person with whom I'm speaking, claiming that I've seen some sort of insect near his ear lobe.

Because there are times when I can't think of anything! But I don't panic. Simply, I look at the person straight on, and cross my eyes. Remember, if you try this the next time you feel awkward in a social situation, it's important to deny that you've crossed your eyes. Continue to act as if everything is "normal."

This will force the other person to think of something to say.

A third and equally effective method for masking any insecurities you might be feeling, is to practice "reflective listening." For instance, if someone says, "I ran into a little traffic on my way over here," the reflective listener will immediately jump in with something along the lines of, "YOU DID? MOTHER OF GOD! YOU POOR THING! I HATE TRAFFIC! TRAFFIC BITES! YOU MUST BE TOTALLY STRESSED OUT AND IN NEED OF A QUALIFIED CHIROPRACTER! HAVE YOU EVER TRIED PILATES? SHOULD I CHECK AND SEE IF THERE IS A FENG SHUI MASTER IN THE HOUSE? THAT COULD REALLY HELP. PEOPLE? EXCUSE ME, PEOPLE? COULD WE GET A LITTLE HELP OVER HERE MOVING THE FURNITURE AROUND? OKAY? LIKE, NOW? WHILE THEY'RE DOING THAT HOW ABOUT I GIVE YOU A NICE FOOT MASSAGE?"

And finally, the trickiest part of party conversation: the Exit.

Sometimes when we're feeling insecure conversing with strangers, we avoid eye contact. Under no circumstance should you *ever* look over someone's shoulder as if you're bored and looking for someone more interesting to talk to. Unless, of course, you're bored and looking for someone more interesting to talk to.

Instead, maintain eye contact and say, simply, "Excuse me, but I believe it's time for my cataract surgery." People tend to let that comment stand on its own. But to end the conversation on a more upbeat tone, you can always add a cheery, "and I'm really looking forward to improved vision!"

Lesson #1: *"Just relax and be yourself," people always say—until you start cleaning your ears at the dinner table. But short of impacted ear wax, it is okay to be yourself.*

Nothing—nothing—is quite as inane as wasting time and energy feeling insecure and intimidated. I take that back. Bruce

Willis movies can sometimes be rather inane. But the point is, indulging those insecure feelings is like keeping yourself in a cage — you're frustrated, you're boxed in, and you just want to hit someone. You feel like a loser because, I'm sorry to say, you're acting like a loser.

I often feel like a loser — but usually only when I'm awake. When I'm asleep, I tend to second-guess myself a lot less.

So, I know. The best way to get over those insecure feelings, then, is to — pardon my gross, but accurate, over-simplification — get over it. Fake it. Jump in. Over and over, until you get tired of stirring up all that adrenaline all the time.

Besides, most people don't really care what you have to say anyway, they're too busy conjuring up their next incredibly un-fascinating, way-too-detailed story.

2

Laugh at Your Vanity

The thing I find fascinating about science—and surely this is what propelled folks like Galileo and Einstein into the field in the first place—is the Law of Bad Looks. It states, simply, that on those days you look especially lousy—mutant hair, gnarled and spotted clothing, red and percolating complexion—you will most certainly run into everyone you have ever known in your entire life.

Conversely, a related axiom maintains that on those days you look spanky, draped in something DKNY-ish, glowing from your recent trip to Barbados, perky, together, on top of the world, there is *absolutely no chance in hell* that you'll run into anyone you know.

Sure, light travels at about 186,000 miles per second, electrons are negatively charged particles, and bears hibernate in the winter. But I ask you, what practical applications does any of this data have?

The Law of Vanity does what science is *supposed* to do: it explains our universe.

It also explains why I run into all the people I've ever known in my entire life, including all previous lives, on days when I look like farm animal droppings. In fact, it's happened so often that I've actually learned to laugh about it. With my therapist. Late at night on an emergency call.

Case in point. There was a time, years ago, when I was in the ladies' room at the shopping mall when I realized, all of a sudden, that I was *really* late for dinner. I rushed out of the bathroom, and started running through the mall, despite the fact that there were some really good shoe sales going on.

Then it dawned on me, as I passed Pottery Barn at a nimble-footed pace, that people were staring. Was it because I was young and pretty? Because my hair was shiny? Because they noticed the athleticism in my sprint? Because they recognized me from a newspaper or magazine picture? Because they liked my outfit, the subtle yet sophisticated way I'd combined stripes and plaids? Because they wanted to be near me, and my kindness, warmth, generosity of spirit, and the torrid heat of my sexual energy?

Two young men stopped in their tracks and stared at me. Hello boys, I projected, having eye-sex with them both. They couldn't take their eyes off me. They were transfixed. They started to smile.

I started to smile.

They started to laugh.

I started to laugh.

They laughed harder.

I laughed harder.

And then it dawned on me. There happened to be an interesting new appendage attached to the top of my jeans, in back, billowing in the wind behind me. A train of *toilet paper*, for the love of God! White, approximately four-feet long—that's *four-feet long*—bouncing along through the mall behind me, my nice, white, two-ply tail.

Let's recap: I was in public with a toilet paper tail approximately the size of a breakfast table flapping behind me. People have joined the monastery for a whole lot less.

Obviously, I didn't join a monastery. The clothes just didn't work, what with all that black and brown. Also, no Diet Coke. So, my friends, I had to laugh. I had to laugh at the situation, at my vanity, at the idiocy of it all. I just had to throw back my head and laugh.

And I did. But not until about four years later.

Friedrich Nietzsche may have said it best: "What is the vanity of the vainest man compared with the vanity which the most modest possesses when, in the midst of nature and the world, he feels himself to be man." You know, I read and reread that line five or six times—not only because of its beauty, its truth, per se, but also because I had absolutely NO IDEA WHATSOEVER what it meant. Was Nietzsche on drugs, or what? I'd like to see Mr. Fred the Know-it-all try to get published these days.

The point is, at the time, my vanity was crushed. The men were not focused on my alleged beauty, sexuality, or athleticism. They were focused on my tail.

So I turned inward. To my studies. I turned to science.

I learned that the speed of sound travels through 32-degree air, at sea level, at about 1088 feet per second. I learned that fungus does not contain chlorophyll.

My mom worried about me. I sensed this because I've always had a special ability to know what people are thinking. An inner eye, if you will. Also, she'd make little comments along the lines of, "Lindsey, I'm worried."

She wanted me to get out more. She sent me new clothes, pretty shoes, encouraged me to get my lip and chin waxed. Which I did. But based on my new, improved packaging, obviously, I saw no one.

The Law of Vanity, and its sister corollaries—The Principle of False Pride and The Law of You're-Not-God's-Gift—were on my mind last week when I ran into an old boyfriend. You know how it is with old flames—you want to look awesome, you want them to lose sleep at night, you want to be way more successful than they are, you want to show them how the split-up catapulted your life into this whole Nirvana state.

And baby, I looked good. Damn good, I'd have to say. Particularly for someone who'd just been thrown up on by a small, but powerfully spew-worthy, baby. Particularly for someone who'd just had a haircut from someone who seemed to be going through some sort of drug withdrawal. Particularly for someone who was skating dangerously close to a deadline and had been up for two solid days.

I'll bet that bad boy lost some sleep that night, but for all the wrong reasons.

Lesson #2: *There's always someone better looking, smarter, richer, and more accomplished than you are. And these are EXACTLY the type of people you want to avoid as friends.*

I'm kidding.

Madonna once said: "I sometimes think I was born to live up to my name. How could I be anything else but what I am having been named Madonna?" So you see? There are people way more screwed up than you are. Way more VAIN. So relax. Laugh at yourself.

Practice not caring how you appear to others. Practice only caring how you appear to really important people. That's not right. Practice remembering how exhausting it is to always put up a front. Remember the starship Enterprise? *Remember how taxing it was to the engines to always have the shields up? Remember how Scotty always tried to freak out James T. by telling him that he needed three days to repair the damage, and then he did it right after the commercial? Remember when I made more sense than Nietzsche?*

The point is, while it's interesting to know that radioactive dating determines the age of an object based on the rates of decay of radioactive isotopes, it's not nearly as useful as knowing that if you happen to see someone you know, perhaps you should quickly duck around the corner. Like a sick, vain coward.

Or you can just stand there and laugh.

3

Laugh at Pretension

Wine. People love to act like they know all about wine.

Correction. People love to act like they know all about everything. I have a friend who is such a pretentious, smug, know-it-all, that he already knows what my next book will be about, even when I don't. The kind of pompous twit who always has to let you know that, no, he hasn't seen the movie, but he's read the book.

Okay, okay, bust me. I've used that line once, too, but only in reference to *The Grinch Who Stole Christmas*.

At a fund-raiser I once met a read-the-book, didn't-see-the-flick man—let's just refer to him as Mr. Fat Head—who felt a need to tell me that he was a really important guy, and spent a lot of time with people like the Justices of the Supreme Court.

"Of the U.S.?" I inquired.

"Sure," Mr. Fat Head said.

"Like at rave parties, or what?" I pressed. "Because the funny thing is, I know one of the Justices. His daughter and I were buddies through high school."

"Huh? Which . . . " That stopped Fat Head cold.

"Billy. Great guy. A lot of fun. Smart, too."

"Rehnquist?!"

"Hi!" I answered, waving to no one in particular in the crowd. And then I laughed heartily, a deep, resonant, James Earl Jones kind of laugh.

Because I despise people like this. People who act like they know everything about everything.

Of course, I *actually* do know quite a bit about "wining and dining"—and I'm not just referring to my ability to argue through an entire dinner.

For instance, I know how to read a wine list, particularly if it's written in English. Also, I can pronounce various names of wines by sophisticatedly saying, "Waiter, I'll have the #24." And I have the confidence, yes I do, to look the wine steward straight in the eye, wink, and inquire, "Tell me, my good man, how much difference is there, *really*, between the chablis and, say, the port?"

But don't feel bad. I used to be just like you, an inept, blubbering schmuck. At restaurants when ordering wine, I often asked the waiter, "What do you have, in terms of wine, that is really, really *filling*?"

Once asked if I preferred white or red, I simply responded, "That depends. Kitchen or bath?"

Of course, all this was *before* I took a wine-tasting class, thank you very much, *before* I subscribed to *The Wine Spectator*, and *before* I moved to one of the premier wine-making regions in the country. Now I act like I'm on intimate terms with any number of wine-making families, ordering the Kendall-Jackson chardonnay, then pretending that my buddies "Ken" and "Jack" were over at the house the other night.

So while you may never be the encyclopedic connoisseur that I am, at least allow me to pass on a few key tips that'll help you look like the pretentious show-off you so powerfully desire to be:

1. Never pronounce a wine's full name. Never say, for example, "I'll have the 1991 Rafanelli Cabernet Sauvignon." Instead say, "I'll have the '91 Raf-Cab." Of course, sometimes this kind of shorthand can confuse an inexperienced waiter when, for instance, you order a "nice chard" and wind up getting a green, leafy vegetable. Remember, if you are served a green, leafy vegetable instead of white wine, by all means, send it back.

2. When ordering wine, be sure to stare at the list for an extremely long period of time, nodding and looking bemused. Then ask the waiter what he recommends. Be sure to respond to the suggestion with: "Actually, my last bottle of that *whatever-you-just-said* was quite high in tannins, but let me try it again." If anyone at the table asks you what tannins are, just pat them on the shoulder, and say, "Come now, I don't want to bore you."

3. When your bottle arrives, do not make a scene by saying, "Waiter! For the love of St. Peter, there's cork in our wine!" Particularly if the bottle has not yet been opened.

4. Look at the wine. Study it. Hold the glass up to the light. Lift the glass up and down several times because, hey, why not get a little exercise? As always, nod slowly, bemusedly.

5. Swirl, then sniff the wine. In our wine-tasting class, my husband swirled his red wine in a manner reminiscent of, say, the Tilt-a-Whirl at a cheap theme park, resulting in the lady next to him looking as if she had been involved in a major traffic accident. Then he inhaled what was left in his glass in a manner not unlike a Hoover vacuum. (Pointer: for etiquette reasons, when you're sniffing, avoid using expletives, or comparisons to out-

houses, wastewater treatment facilities, or Superfund sites. Instead, comment on "the lovely aroma" and "the delightful bouquet.")

6. Sip and swish. Gently. Remember, this is a restaurant, not a Listerine commercial. "Swirl" the wine around on your "tongue," theatrically closing your "eyes" as you do "so."

7. Swallow and comment. Remember, this is your opportunity to sound like a thesaurus gone rabid: "Ahhh . . . physical, yet cerebral. Whimsical, yet fundamental. Spontaneous, yet organized. Meaty, yet vegetarian, maybe even vegan." And *always* comment on the "overtones" and "balance" as in, "You know, this wine sure has some serious overtones and balance."

Of course, if the wine is bad, you'll have to send it back. Be pleasant with your waiter. After all, he wasn't monitoring the residual sugar when the grapes were picked. Tell him exactly why you're sending the wine back—such as, "You call this zinfandel? I'm afraid I'll have to send it back! Why, it tastes like—like—RED WINE!"

Lesson #3: *If you can't beat 'em, join 'em. If someone at your table starts acting like Mr. Fancy Pants Wine Master, grab the wine list and maintain control. Make the comment, to no one in particular, "GOD! IT'S REALLY SOMETHING THEY'RE DOING WITH FRENCH OAK THESE DAYS!" Later, take out your platinum card. And photos of yourself at a White House dinner. Refer to Candice Bergen as "Candy." Complain about how hard it is to find decent household help.*

Yikes. That's wrong. What am I saying?

Don't be sucked down to the level of some pretentious twerp. Go the other way.

For instance, if the waiter brings olive oil with the bread, ask for margarine. No. Ask for vegetable shortening. Try, "Do you think you could round up a little Crisco? When you get a minute? Thanks, Amigo." And then carry on with the conversation. Pretentious people get very uncomfortable when they are in uncertain waters. But always show class. When the Crisco arrives, pass it around, politely offering, "Lard, anyone?"

4

Laugh at Your Shortcomings

"You're late," our hosts said as we arrived at their home, a little overdue, for dinner. "Traffic?"

No.

"Car trouble?"

No.

"Get lost?"

Perhaps. But only in the metaphysical sense.

They stared at us, "Well?"

"We're late," I said, "We're late because . . . we're *polite*." Then I laughed to diffuse the tension in the air. I laughed to show them that a few minutes late is not the end of the world. I laughed because other guests were putting on their coats, having finished their dinners and heading for the front door.

Oh sure, we all have shortcomings. Shoot, even members

of my own family have shortcomings. For instance, they don't always think I'm right. My husband has short-comings, because he doesn't always think I'm right. My editor has shortcomings, because he doesn't always think I'm right.

Not that I don't have a whole list of shortcomings, myself. For instance, I'm opinionated, but with good reason. I laugh at what others perceive as inappropriate times, but who said funeral and city council meetings should be so grim. I'm short-tempered, because I hate to waste time. I'm impatient, because I'm short-tempered. I'm critical, because folks tend to strike me as highly flawed.

But I'm not rude. If I were rude, I'd always be on time.

Sometimes folks don't appreciate that. They don't fully grasp the concept of "lateness," with all its intricacies, all its ramifications.

Airlines, for example. They don't get it. They respond to my well-mannered lateness by leaving me at the gate.

Restaurants often misinterpret my act of etiquette by theatrically looking at their watches, huffing and puffing as if they'd just finished the Boston marathon, whispering among themselves, then leading me to the table right under the leaking pipe.

And once when I arrived late for a job interview, the person with whom I was interviewing not only seemed unimpressed with me, she seemed annoyed. "Well, can you tell me anything *good* about yourself?" she asked.

"Sure, you bet," I said. "For one thing, I don't rush people, or make them feel frazzled. Also, I don't tailgate."

My whole family is thoughtful this way, especially my brother, who is so courteous that friends and family have started lying to him. Telling him that the party starts at 5:00, when it really starts at 7:00, that the dinner reservations are at 6:30, when they're really at 8:30.

My younger sister used to always arrive late to class, too, and only, in part, due to the fact that she was quite fond of sleeping in. The other part of it, make no mistake, is that she wanted to provide the professor ample time to prepare for the lecture.

But not wanting to draw attention to her exceptional behavior—which in itself seems terribly polite to me—she downplayed the late arrival by limping to her chair, once borrowing her roommate's crutch, or acting like she had a bad nosebleed.

Now that's good manners—plus a large helping of panache.

Fortunately, I learned this lesson about lateness long ago, when guests arrived half an hour early for a dinner party at our house.

What's *that* about?! Never come early to my house. Never. Don't hurt me like that. Because if you want to be rude, or hurt my feelings, why not just plug your nose while eating my culinary concoctions, periodically snorting like some sort of swine, and occasionally buckling over and screaming out in acute gastrointestinal pain.

I was in the kitchen when the doorbell rang.

In the kitchen, in my underwear, a green moisturizing mask on my face, white styling goop on my hair, army boots from the First World War on my feet. Little Ms. Haute Couture.

The doorbell rang and there was absolutely no way for me to get upstairs from the kitchen without sashaying directly in front of the window where the early, and therefore barbaric, savages stood.

Quick. Options. Could I drape myself with pot-holders? Yes. If only I had about fifty of them.

Could I use the kitchen fire extinguisher to create a cloud of fog around me, David Copperfield–like, and scamper by the window camouflaged as a cumulus cloud? Maybe.

Perhaps I could urge one of my dogs to take a message upstairs to my husband who, due to some rare neurological condition, never hears the doorbell ring. The message would urge him to bring clothes, or a bathrobe.

You can imagine my disappointment when I realized that this wasn't an episode of *Lassie*.

Finally I took a section of the newspaper, opened it up, and walked by that window. Two bare legs, and the classifieds.

Since that night, not only have I put curtains over that window, which I keep pulled closed all the time, and scratched those Premature Primates out of my little black book, I've sworn *never* to be on time.

I'm just too polite.

Lesson #4: *All good things come to those who wait.*

Furthermore, people who arrive early, or let's go so far as to say, on time, to any event, tend to exhibit strong qualities of loserhood. I mean this in the nicest way possible. They're the sort of high-strung individuals who get their Christmas cards out in time for Christmas, have their towels monogrammed, and take pride in their organized sock drawers.

Can you imagine your own life being so devoid of all meaning, so pointless, that you actually take time to organize your blasted sock drawer? Or even have a drawer that is specifically allocated for socks?

Show some compassion for these sad, empty people. Cheer them up, share a laugh. Because they're just not right in the head.

5

Laugh at Society

I've always seen myself as a simple person with simple needs—a decent pair of shoes, a simple roof over my head, sufficient food on the table, a huge, 200-foot-long yacht with a helicopter pad on top, a national holiday named in my honor—but recently I learned something new about myself.

I have a benign growth on my shoulder that needs to be removed.

Also, I learned that in order to be accepted as a pillar of "society"—and by this I mean, basically, a Stuck-Up Self-Assured Major-Idiot Snob, as opposed to a more pedestrian definition of the word—one must get into a number of areas.

One must have household help. One must call one's babysitter a "nanny." One must suggest allowing a bottle of wine to "open up." One must enroll one's children in at least 47 activities, including Baroque Painting for three-year-olds and semi-private Far East cooking classes.

And one must know, understand, and do auctions.

Not the eBay, Bid.com, HaggleZone internet kind of auctions where you can get a "Proven Metaphysical Lottery System" for $9.99, a three-piece drum kit for $250, or a pathetic and truly strange Hummel figure for under $100, but real, live auctions. Where you can sip champagne, eat crepes and caviar, and view masterpieces of art, antiques, and jewelry.

Where else can you chew the fat with the elite, pick up a $50,000 bottle of wine, spend $48,000 for Jackie O's tape measure, $772,500 for a set of golf clubs, or *hundreds* of dollars on a doghouse?

Okay, if that had been an SAT question, which item wouldn't have fit?

The doghouse was exactly the item up for bid when I decided to get a little big for my britches. Hell, the money was for charity, I kept repeating like some sort of drunken debutante. My bidding on a dog house would benefit one of my favorite non-profit organizations which provides trained dogs for people with disabilities, Canine Companions for Independence.

Never mind that my dogs live, eat, sleep, and periodically relieve themselves inside my house. It was for charity!

Oh sure, at first, I was reluctant to bid. I was thinking about my phone bill and, specifically, about the fact that I hadn't actually paid it.

And then I got mad. Everyone else was having all the fun. I thought, "WHY LET THE STUPID PHONE COMPANY RULE MY LIFE, DAMNIT?!"

But I was a little intimidated. I'd never bid on anything in my life. In fact, including my entire educational years, I'd almost never raised my hand.

But doggonit, I got mad again! I thought, "Since *when* am

I afraid of making a total fool of myself in public, where people look and laugh and point?!" Laugh at society, I always say. Laugh at all the contrived, attention-starved behaviors of those who play this showy little game.

Laugh at myself, in other words. I jumped right in. I raised my hand. Unfortunately, the auction hadn't actually *started* yet.

To camouflage my awkwardness, I pretended to be stretching. I repeated several more arm raises, stretching side to side, and added a few deep knee bends for authenticity.

Eventually, the auctioneer walked onto the stage. He looked bemused, smug even, as if he was used to working a crowd, piece of cake, no sweat, baby, and started speaking in that fast, grating, unrelenting auctioneer voice that makes me wish I'd applied for a concealed weapon license.

"Do I hear two hundred dollars for this beautiful yamma-yacka-yadda doghouse up here? Do I hear two hundred dollars? Two hundred dollars for the macka-yadda-badda . . . "

"What?" someone asked. "What'd he just say?"

"Do-we-have two hundred dollars, do-I-hear-a-two-hundred-dollar-humdigga-wacka-dacka . . . "

That voice, I felt certain, was starting to give me brain damage, and truly, I felt compelled to protect what little I had left. I decided to shove my hand into the air.

"Not your HAND!" my husband hissed, looking embarrassed by my idiocy, like he needed to issue the crowd a formal apology. "You're supposed to use a paddle."

Ah, a *paddle*. It's protocol to use paddles, apparently. And you can certainly see why. Paddles are for ping pong and . . . uh . . . auctions. Right. I got it now. I put my paddle in the sky and started swinging it madly in the air like Venus Williams.

"I've got two hundred dollars-bugga-bugga. Do I see three hundred? Do I mucka-mucka-see three hundred, three hundred, three hundred . . . ?"

My EARS! That VOICE! My EARS! That VOICE! My hand rocketed into the air, once again.

"LINDSEY! You're bidding against YOURSELF!" my husband hissed again.

"Right. Well, I've always been my own worst enemy," I hissed back. I raised my hand again. And again. "How about four-fifty?" I offered. "Are we up to four hundred fifty yet? Or maybe five hundred?"

"I-see-three-hundred-we've-got three-hundred. Do-I-see-four-hundred-four-hundred-four-hundred? Do-I-see-boom-shocka-shocka-shocka . . ."

I scanned the crowd, my adversaries. A man offered a bid. SWINE! Someone else made another bid! FIEND! Another malcontent upped the ante even higher! VILLAIN! Yet another warmonger was vying for a piece of the action!

I was being ambushed.

Going once, going twice . . .

Hors d'oeuvres and bubbly. Fine art, heirlooms, jewels, extravagance. Auctions are all the rage these days.

Lesson #5: *Laugh at your feeble attempts to be cool and part of "society." Laugh at the idiots around you who, seemingly, have it all figured out. Money doesn't buy happiness; it buys doghouses. Just like the really gigantic one sitting, unused, out in my driveway.*

6

Laugh at All of Life's Changes

It was our last night in Hawaii, and we were enjoying the sunset. Piña coladas in hand, my husband and I sat on a grassy spot in front of the beach, leaning back against a palm tree, his arm wrapped around me. A gentle breeze filled the air with intoxicating floral fragrances. The sunset cast a brilliant, magical glow over our lovebird world.

Sorry. For a minute I thought I was employed by Hallmark.

"This is indescribable," he said.

"Thoroughly," I responded. Because, for one thing, as this romantic, Hollywood-perfect scene was taking place, the baby was simultaneously using my legs as a jungle gym. Tugging at my shorts and shirtsleeves. Pulling up impressively large sections of lawn. Looking for really dirty things to put in his mouth. All the while, happily chirping, "Ma? Da? Mama! Da!"

It was a moment of sudden insight, and I'm not referring to the fact that it had just become explosively clear that the little guy needed an immediate diaper change.

It had also become clear that parenting knows no vacations.

In fact, forget about morning sickness, labor and delivery, squished, strangely shaped heads, diaper rash, teething, and sleepless nights. You aren't really a parent until you've taken your first parent-child vacation.

The first parent-child vacation. The one when your little darling insists upon pushing the broom he's found behind the valet's counter in front of the nice, expensive hotel where you are blowing all your savings. The one where you allow him to push the blasted broom, because it is making him so rip-roaringly happy, and because it seems harmless.

The vacation where you realize that your child is now ramming the broom into the nice, expensive shoes of the nice hotel guests who, by the way, don't seem like the sort of people who have a stash of peanut butter and jelly up in their rooms, or who schlep a week's supply of juice boxes wherever they go.

The vacation where you engage in such relaxed and frivolous lost-in-paradise banter as:

"Sweetheart, let's put the nice broom away now so we can go find daddy..."

"*ARRGHHH!!!*"

"Okay. Mommy is going to take the nice broom now, and put..."

"*EEEEEEEE!!!*"

"The broom has to go bye-bye so that..."

"*NOOOOOO!!!*"

"Bye-bye Mr. Nice Broom, we have to..."

What's more, you aren't really a parent until you're in the

lobby of the aforementioned hotel and your child performs a PDNM, or Public Display Nuclear Meltdown.

It was fascinating. It was spirited. It was even potentially *profitable*. Because, I want to tell you, tourists gathered as if this were just one more fascinating aspect of the island's rich cultural life.

Hawaii's Half-pint, Hardheaded Hula Boy.

And finally, you aren't really a parent until your young child manages, somehow, to climb up onto the miniature stage at a local restaurant where you are attempting to dine, in order to more thoroughly examine all the interesting knobs on the band's amplifying equipment.

The vacation where you leap like a wide receiver to intercept your child before he can actually electrify himself and/or get you arrested.

So much for sleeping in. So much for midnight walks along the beach. So much for elegant dinners out. Vacations will never be quite the same.

In fact, they'll be better.

Because frankly, I've never had so much fun. I've never laughed so hard as when the baby walked around the pool area greeting sunbathers with his two favorite words: "*Hi!*" and "*Moo!*"

Or when he chased his beach ball, tried to do a hula dance, heard pounding drums at a luau, and had his first taste of papaya.

And never have I laughed so much at life as I did during our last evening in Hawaii, my husband and I snuggled together on a grassy patch under a palm tree, gazing wondrously at this spectacular sunset, Jack busy unlacing our shoes.

Lesson #6: *Times change, and we all change with time. Since we can't stop the process, we should sit back and marvel at it.*

OR

Alternative Lesson #6: *Stay at a hotel with one of those kid camps.*

OR

Second Alternative Lesson #6: *Don't wear lace-up shoes.*

PART II

EMBRACE LIFE'S CHALLENGES

Picture this. I'm out in the back yard throwing a tennis ball around for one of my dogs. She brings it to me, I tell her to "drop it." She is not obedient, so she does not "drop it." Nonetheless, I repeat the command several times, finally wrestling it out of her mouth. I give the now-disgusting slime ball an impressive heave-ho.

My dog goes scampering off after it. But, as is often the case, she picks up on some All-Powerful Mystery Scent en route, which then has her charging, sniffing, around every tree and shrub in my back yard like some sort of rabid maniac.

The ball is in plain sight. But no. She's racing to the maple tree, tongue and ears flapping in the wind.

"*It's right there!*" I shout, pointing. She's circling the other side of the yard now. "RIGHT THERE!" I yell. She looks at me as if I've lost my mind.

There are two possible conclusions we can draw from this scenario:

1. Like my tongue-flapping dog, most of us spend a lot of time following the wrong scent. The ball, if we stop being so blasted distracted, is right there, and;

2. I have certainly gone to a lot of trouble to set up an analogy that is questionable at best.

The point, though, is this. Self-help sections in bookstores and libraries are full of books on success, happiness, perfect love, perfect relationships, inner peace, problem solving, and how to "have it all." Pop psychology is about making everything nice and tidy.

This, it strikes me, is a major disservice.

Because the truth is, regular lives are filled with a truly astounding number of screw-ups and bunglings. "Challenges," we could call them. Challenges aren't the exception, as so many of us have been led to believe, they're the rule, the natural condition. Challenges are part of the fabric. They're intrinsic. So rather than attempting to rid ourselves of these "challenges," perhaps we should simply embrace them.

While drinking heavily.

7

Embrace Your Hamhocks

I'm trying to embrace my masculine side.

Which isn't to say that I'm leaving my shoes in the middle of the floor, or publicly adjusting the crotch of my pants, or playing rock 'n' roll music on an imaginary electric guitar, or telling my spouse: "That ridiculous—you're overreacting."

It means, simply, that I'm trying to become more comfortable running around public pools in my swimsuit.

You know, like a man.

It's the naked truth. When it comes to feeling just fine about cavorting around in the semi-buff, men are way ahead of women.

Oh sure, we all have our challenging physical traits. Our hair is too unmanageable, our faces too broken out, our body odor is too putrid, our teeth are too yellow. But enough about me.

So, I'm trying to embrace the fact that, for instance, my butt has its own website. I'm not trying to change it; I'm trying to embrace it. Which, as you can imagine, takes a lot more flexibility than I currently have in stock. I'd pretty much have to be triple-jointed, or something.

I'm not alone. A girl friend of mine has flabby arms. She exercises, eats right, and wears flattering sleeve lengths. Talk about a hysterical reaction!

Another friend is self-conscious about his over-bite. Which is ridiculous. Even if he does look like Gomer Pyle. I tell him that if he's ever held at gun-point, he can just turn toward his attacker and lean forward.

Another friend, a woman, has decided to compensate for her height—and I'm not kidding, she's like a friggin' giraffe—by stooping over like the Hunchback of Notre Dame.

"Embrace your physical self!" I tell them all, sucking in my tummy. "Don't try so hard to be something you're not."

So, as far as the whole female butt-and-thigh thing go, I'm trying to be more like a man. Men don't care if they're wearing a non-detachable inner-tube, or whether they're paler than Michael Jackson. They don't worry about underwires, or the advantages of stripes versus bold floral, or whether the length of their swim trunks is flattering to their thighs.

And while there's always the exception to the rule—like the Rhode Island man who shot a guy at a bar who, according to police, had called him "fatso"—most men don't care. They buy swimsuits when they can't find their old ones—and WITHOUT EVEN TRYING THEM ON!

"Where did you get those things?" I recently asked my husband when he sauntered outside in red swim trunks with little panda bears all over them. The sort of scintillating fashion statement that had me reaching for antacid.

"Huh? Oh. I dunno," he said, slouched over. "I just found them in a drawer."

"You don't know?" I persisted. "And do you have to slouch like that? Don't you worry about your posture?"

"I've decided to embrace my lousy posture," he answered.

"You know what?" I said, now annoyed that anyone could so *easily* embrace his physical challenges. "Those panda bear trunks make you look like an idiot."

And to think of all the happy time I spend on my swimsuit purchases. Alone, in an over-heated and cramped dressing room, in bad lighting, with an excessive number of mirrors, providing an excessive number of angles, on an excessive amount of flesh.

Not that I don't look good in a swimming suit. Actually, I look *great* at the pool, at the beach, swimming around in the water. Particularly if you love marine mammals. And here I'm thinking about *Free Willy*.

"What are you contemplating so seriously, Lindsey?" my husband recently asked me. "Are you thinking about the beginning of the Universe, and why matter fought antimatter for eternal dominance?"

"Pretty much."

"Are you thinking about why some worms, seeking protection from predators, evolved into clams and scallops?"

"That was yesterday."

"Well, then, are you thinking about how Plato, who was a student of Socrates, later became the teacher of Aristotle?"

"I'm thinking about my butt," I said.

"What about it, exactly?"

"How it reminds me of the Red Roof Inn."

"In what way?"

"SIZE."

"That's ridiculous," he said. "You're overreacting."

Hmmm.

Which is why, short of back hair, I'm trying to embrace my masculine side. I'm not going to be such a self-conscious and silly *girl* about it.

Next time I'm around a pool, I'm going to focus on what's really important in life: Jumping! Splashing! Family fun and games!

Did anyone say cover-ups?

Lesson #7: *Blubber is good. Marine mammals, which have been around a lot longer than humankind, wouldn't have survived without that all-important layer of blubber.*

Unfortunately, however, more than half of us—54.3 per-cent—would rather get run over by a truck than gain 150 pounds. I read that in a book. Fortunately, these aren't the only two op-tions.

Another option might be to try to make friends with some really fat people, and start hanging out with them. Another op-tion might be to skip the pool scene.

I'm kidding. Life's too short for this sort of self-absorbed obsession with our bodies. Embrace your hamhocks, just think of what a great, big splash you can make.

8

Embrace Your Fear

Some people increase their dietary fiber, or drink prune juice, or try over-the-counter remedies such as Ex-Lax. But take it from me, for that occasional bout of irregularity, nothing works better than a dose of public speaking.

Especially if you happen to catch a cold the morning of the event, so your voice sounds like a biting cross between Fran Drescher and Brenda Vaccaro.

There's so much to fear in life!

Disease, high cholesterol, and death. Some people are afraid they'll run out of money. Lots of folks fear for the health, safety, and general well-being of their children while, at the same time, contemplating ways to send the little stinkers off to military school.

There are people who have a fear of heights, or of closed places, or of open places. Some people are afraid to go to the dentist. And if you're like me, you've got a fear of being enclosed, in a high place, with a dentist.

Lots of people have a fear of flying. Again, like me. I have a fear of flying compounded by a HORRIBLE fear of hearing people tell me, over and over, "Well, you know what? It's a lot safer than driving." Gee, I'd never heard that before. I guess I'm cured!

My son fears monsters, my daughter is afraid of two food items coming in contact with each other on the same plate, and my dogs fear vacuum cleaners. Which is on my list, too. Also, sometimes I'm afraid of the world ending in a fiery ball of exploding matter. But this usually coincides with family reunions.

Family reunions not withstanding, public speaking is, statistically, everyone's major fear. And I was reminded of its marvelous colon-clearing powers, recently, when I gave a little talk for the Spokane Junior League. This was shortly after my column had been picked up by the Spokane newspaper, and I was on a whirlwind media junket to promote myself in that town.

Fortunately, the Spokane Junior League is packed full of the nicest women you could ever hope to meet. And fortunately, I'd done enough public speaking to know that the increased heart rate, shortness of breath, chest pains, short bouts of unconsciousness, and episodes of CPR by highly-trained emergency ambulance staff were all normal.

So I comforted myself with the fact that what Americans fear *most*—more than snakes, heights, disease, financial ruin, overly attentive waiters, and Arnold Schwarzenegger movies—is speaking before a group. Fear of public speaking even outranks the fear of *death*.

Resolutely, then, I dismissed the memory of my first speech—way back in seventh grade when I managed, single-handedly, to launch most members of my audience into temporary comas.

I blocked the memory of the preventive Kleenex I'd crammed into my marshy armpits prior to that speech—Kleenex which fell when I walked to the podium, one wad to my waist, so it looked like I had some kind of advanced tumor, the other to the floor where I tried to kick it, soccer-like, behind the podium.

I chose not to dwell on the fact that my speech started with the scintillating lines: "My name is Lindsey Stokes, I'm not here to tell jokes. I'd like to make it evident, I'm running for vice-president." Because, hey, the silver lining of that idiotic kind of writing is—it resulted in a professional writing career!

Instead, I focused on the fact that I'd successfully given lots of speeches.

Okay, maybe "successfully" is something of a reach, especially if you consider the time my husband accompanied me to an afternoon conference, where I was one of many speakers. The audience was tired when I started, and so my husband, who is as technically gifted as a shoehorn, got the big idea to turn the auditorium lights up to full brightness.

He hit the wrong switches. What we in the auditorium got instead of a properly illuminated room was a pulsating, strobe-lighted Michael Jackson concert hall with the overhead lights alternating between brightness, darkness, and back again.

For years after that, I suffered from post-traumatic stress disorder. Whenever I saw blinking lights—whether at traffic intersections or on Christmas trees—I withdrew into the fetal position. Eventually, I tried to embrace the Christmas lights.

Now I have a fear of third-degree burns.

Lesson #8: *Recognize your fear, feel it. It feels like hell, doesn't it? Okay. Try saying to yourself, over and over, "I'm scared to death, my stomach is churning, and it feels like hell." Now, do you feel better?*

Of course you don't.

Because the secret to overcoming fear is not merely to feel it, but to embrace it. To do exactly that which tests the limitations of your anti-perspirant. The more times you manage to face your fear and work your way through it, the more you'll feel in control of your life and destiny. Which, of course, you are not. Also, you'll have acquired an impressive collection of anti-perspirants.

9

Embrace Chaos

Few things are more fun than spending an evening dining out with young children—although dental procedures involving high-powered drills, and head-on collisions with tractor-trailers, are two that come immediately to mind.

Life is full of chaos. The rush hour is chaos, malls before and after Christmas are chaos, every aspect of airline travel is chaos, my hair is chaos.

Henry B. Adams once said, "Chaos often breeds life, when order breeds habit." It's a brilliant, profound, and inspiring thought, which leads me to believe that Henry never went out to dinner with young kids.

The most important aspect of successful (and fun!) restaurant dining with the young terrorists, then, is to plan ahead. Specifically, you should be in shape and have had some survival training with the Marines. Also, you should have a map. For finding a faraway town where you can enjoy your lovely meal without the possibility of running into anyone you know.

There are good reasons for being anonymous.

"I really enjoy your column," someone once said to me in a Denver restaurant. "I think that . . . " PHWACK! A whole-grain roll pelted her in the arm.

"Kids!" I hissed under my breath, squinting menacingly at them like Cruella DeVille. "Thank you so much," I said, turning back to the woman, as I attempted to smile and appear gracious, while simultaneously kicking one of the kids under the table for blowing bubbles into her milk.

An additional bonus of anonymous dining is that close friends and neighbors don't get to see you acting like a congenital idiot playing little games with Mr. and Mrs. Salt and Pepper Shaker. They won't witness the Shaker couple dancing around the butter dish. They won't see you getting your face right down in front of Mr. Pepper and saying, "Well, hello there, Mr. Pepper-man. We're awfully glad you could join us for dinner!" They won't see Mr. Pepper and Mrs. Salt giving each other a big kiss.

Another advantage of dining with your family in a remote, uninhabited town is that friends, neighbors, and individuals with whom you might have professional contact won't have the opportunity to see you, a grown human being who actually votes in presidential elections, actually blowing straw wrappers across the table.

Also, they won't see you eating with all the poise and grace of Conan the Barbarian. Because when you're out to eat with kids, the key factor is *not* ambience, my friend, or service, or the intricacies of sophisticated food preparation.

The key factor is *speed*. Actually chewing is not required.

"*We're ready to order!*" I often shout from the parking lot, before we've actually entered the restaurant. "*And we need more napkins! And straws. Also, could you bring us the check? And more napkins!*"

Oh gosh, remember the days when you actually conversed while dining? When there was communication? You chatted about movies,   literature, interesting world events. And you tasted the food. Savored it, even, wondering which seasonings might have contributed to which flavors.

Ha! Who's got time for all that extracurricular frivolity when there are hundreds of small, multi-colored sugar packets to pick up off the floor?

In fact, between the mopping, the juggling, the continual requests for extra napkins, and the picking up, I usually feel as if I'm working off my dinner as I'm eating it.

Which is why some people—intelligent, rational people— prefer NOT to eat out with their children, contending that it's "not worth the effort."

Pity. Life goes so fast. What an unbecoming attitude. Because for the rest of us—and by that I mean, those of us who could not line up babysitters—we believe that Friday night is family night. And we're going to have some rollicking good weekend fun out on the town, as a family, even if it kills us.

So, please, allow me to offer the following helpful advice for you wonderfully masochistic families:

1. Bring lots of toys to the restaurant. Your child will not play with these toys. He'll fuss and whine until you hand him your pager, or your wallet, or your purse, and then he'll proceed to dump it out with the sugar packets. But bringing the toys will make you feel like a better parent;

2. Don't worry about what your child eats. In fact, save yourself a whole lot of trouble and simply order her a bowl of ketchup;

3. Be sure to move all unnecessary items from the table, and by this I mean plates, forks, knives, water glasses, table cloths, bread baskets and anything else that this "family-un-friendly" restaurant has thoughtlessly left on the table, and;

4. Tip heavily. You won't feel so guilty about the fact that your waiter will now require a couple of weeks in the Caribbean, and that the food-littered area under your table looks like some sort of nuclear device just went off.

Lesson #9: *Life is chaotic. The most important method for embracing chaos, then, is to drink heavily. Have I said that before? Are you starting to think that I may have a problem? Is it so wrong to start drinking way before the cocktail hour? Before lunch? First thing in the morning?*

I'm talking about water here, of course. And all the amazing health and psychological benefits eight glasses of water can give you in one day.

So what if life is chaotic? The alternative to chaos is boredom. And chaos is a relative thing—just think, before you know it, your kids will go from tossing rolls across the table to using drugs and engaging in pre-marital sex. This restaurant stuff will seem like a day in the park.

Lesson #9A: *Did anyone say* carry-out?

Lesson #9B: *Did anyone say* babysitter?

10

Embrace Your Awkwardness

At a large gathering of family and friends a few years ago, I was called upon to give a toast. Naturally, I was more than happy to oblige—until I realized that they weren't talking about cooked bread.

"Oh, you want me to say something? Something clever and witty, sincere and heartfelt, something possibly even inspiring?" I asked. Fine. No problem. I'm a trained professional.

So I cleared my throat five or six times, cracked my knuckles, rubbed my palms together, stretched, took some deep breaths.

"GOD—what is this—*an exercise video*?" my sister asked.

Life is full of awkward moments. So, after mopping my forehead with a section of the linen tablecloth, I regained my composure and looked at all the expectant faces turned my way. "Let's raise our glasses—" I started to say . . .

"Let's rate our *asses*? Now why ON EARTH would we want to do a thing like that?" my Aunt Carrie asked, a person who had, apparently, already been toasting. "Because mine's as big as a building."

"No, no, let's raise our *glasses*," I clarified. "I'd like to propose a toast."

And then, purely for lack of a better idea, I said, "May a band of gypsies pierce your noses, and may trained bears dance on your heads."

It was weird. Not as weird, perhaps, as the fact that a woman who once won the Mrs. Congeniality Award at the Mrs. New York state beauty pageant was arrested for punching and kicking a cop and landing him in the hospital. But still. Weird.

The point is, life is full of awkward moments. The first time we try anything new—a sport, a hobby, a new language— we feel awkward. Like total spastic idiots. So we try it again. Okay, we're still feeling awkward. We try again, and again. Oops. Still awkward.

All people feel awkward. If you don't believe that, you haven't ridden on an elevator lately. You haven't taken a class where the teacher has you go around the room, each person saying a little something about him or herself. You haven't stood in the lobby of a really nice, expensive, crowded hotel lobby and had your dog pee on the floor.

We've all tripped or stumbled in front of people, and felt like idiots. We've all come across an acquaintance, not remembered her name, and felt like an idiot. We've all been at a dinner party, gone off to use the bathroom, only to have the toilet back up.

We've all experienced that horror when the toilet starts overflowing onto the floor in one gigantic septic mess. We've all stood there while the men at the party, alleged plumbers all, have gone in and out of the bathroom, each time feeling the need to comment on the obscene septic mess. We've all had that happen, haven't we? We haven't? You mean, just me?

Septic mishaps notwithstanding, it's always awkward to offer a toast.

At my best friend's wedding reception, for example, I stood in front of the happy crowd and said, profoundly and articulately, "Uh, yeah, okay. I just wanted to say that . . . you know . . . these guys up here . . . what with the wedding and all . . . I just think that . . . with getting married and everything like that . . . uh . . . that they will always be . . . uh . . . you know."

And at a luncheon celebrating my sister's college graduation, I raised my glass in her direction and said, "May the years ahead of you be prosperous, fruitful ones, and may you, in turn, prosper fruitfully in the various, and what-not, fruitful years ahead of your own fruitful self."

And finally, at a business dinner prior to a speech I was giving in Kansas City, I said, "Basically, I'd just like to thank basically everyone here that, uh, I should be thanking, by saying, basically, thank you. To everyone. I should be thanking."

"I need to improve my toasts," I told a friend of mine who specializes in public speaking.

"Have you tried jam?" she asked. "That always works for me. And there's always cinnamon and sugar."

"No, *toasts*—you know, the custom that originated with the Greeks in the sixth century B.C. in order to assure guests that the wine they were about to drink was not poisoned which, at the time, was something they tended to run into a lot."

Fortunately, she gave me a few tips:

1. Offer the toast in a way that is most comfortable for you unless, of course, that involves leaning back in your chair and putting your feet up on the table while patting your belly like ol' St. Nick and belching at random;

2. Don't combine toasts with other pieces of information.

For instance, at your New Year's Eve dinner, don't say, "Here's to the year 2001, and could someone give me a ride to the store tomorrow, and *Seinfeld* is on in twenty minutes"; and finally,

3. In case you're called on unexpectedly, always be prepared to offer an appropriate toast by memorizing a few all-purpose ones ahead of time. "Bottoms up!" and "Down the hatch!" are two that come immediately to mind, and ones I've used at occasions ranging from church dinners to business lunches.

Lesson #10: *Life is full of awkward moments. If we cringe at them, if we're horrified by them, they can ruin our lives. Whenever you find yourself in an awkward moment, embrace it. For instance, if at a party you see someone whose name you cannot remember, exclaim, "Oh, God! I've forgotten your name AGAIN! You must not be all that important to me."*

And remember, when offering a toast, whatever you say is going to be a whole lot better than the time, back in December 1982, when President Ronald Reagan stood at a dinner hosted in his honor by the president of Brazil and proposed a toast to "the people of Bolivia."

11

Embrace Life's Passages

In January, people are looking forward to spring. In spring, they're looking forward to summer. In summer, they're looking forward to fall. In fall, they're looking forward to Christmas.

Life is full of significant, important, meaningful rites of passages. The first time we walk, the first time we head off to school, the first time we kiss someone, the first time we have a beer, the first time we bring the car home late, the first time we get finger-printed by the FBI.

Good God. Shouldn't we enjoy each day, each phase of our lives, as it happens?

For instance, one of the many joys, glories, and wonders of parenthood is that, at some point, you find yourself, a college graduate and someone who pays taxes and votes in all major elections, gazing into the eyes of your precious, darling offspring and saying, in a positive—but not pushy—manner, "Is the *pee-pee* coming yet?"

And yes, I've found myself having a quiet evening at home with the family, sitting around watching a little video in which a small, anatomically correct cartoon figure talks about his penis, and how useful it is when it comes to the task of making, and I'm quoting here, *"wee-wee."*

I've lived a long time and seen a lot of things, and *still* I'm not all that comfortable talking about, much less using the word, *"wee-wee."*

But it could be worse. I know this. We could be watching the *other* video—the one where all the nice farm animals are happily defecating, while the *way-too-cheerful* announcer brightly describes the action: "Look! There's Mr. Horsey making a nice B.M! Good boy, Mr. Horsey! Good B.M.! And look! The little white goat is making some wee-wee! Good wee-wee, little Miss White Goat..."

Please.

Perhaps even more disturbing than all this, our child has shown an uncharacteristic ability to focus for *lengthy periods of time* on these videos, often bringing them out when adult guests are in the house, often repeating his favorite lines to them.

"Why can't he just stay in diapers until he's forty?" my husband asked.

"I don't have a problem with that," I said.

But, alas, we want to do right by our children. We don't want kids teasing him in the high school locker room because he's still in Pampers. We don't want him squatting in the middle of the dance floor, at his senior prom, with that strange little far-off, but concentrated, look in his eye while, as the cheerful video narrator might put it, he makes a nice—well, you know.

Mostly, though, we don't want him writing books about us.

Which is why, in undertaking the task of potty-training,

we consulted Dr. T. Berry Brazelton, Dr. Spock, Captain Kirk, Penelope Leach, *Webster's Collegiate Dictionary* (Tenth Edition), the horoscope, the long-range weather forecast, and the daily stock index prices, and wrote letters to our Congressional representatives.

What we learned was this: Mess up on the potty training, folks, and your kid grows up to be the sort of maladjusted psycho who honks at other drivers and sneaks too many items into the grocery store express checkout lane.

We were scared.

Nonetheless, we knew this was one of life's passages. So we embraced it.

"This is a potty seat," I told my son, using my best, positive, non-threatening voice. "You sit right here," I added, waving at the potty seat in a manner reminiscent of Vanna White, "and you go—ahem—*poo-poo* and, uh, *pee* right here."

He seemed to catch right on. In fact, he took the removable container out of the potty seat, and put it on his head.

"Hat," he said.

"What a good boy! What a good boy!" I raved, supporting him emotionally and remaining positive. "Okay. Let's say Mr. Pee Container is tired of being a hat, what's he going to do? 'I've got it,' Mr. Pee Container says, 'I'll get right back in this potty seat and hope someone gives me some poo-poo and pee.'"

This was getting sick.

"Poo-poo and pee?" my young diaper-clad friend asked.

"Yes! *Yes*, my darling!"

He studied the container, then looked at me.

"Mommy go pee in there!"

Hmmm. Not what I had in mind.

"Mommy go poo-poo in there!" He seemed to be on to something.

I needed to think fast. I needed all my expertise, knowledge, and training as a parent, combined with my good instincts and intellect, to handle this tricky situation.

"Okay. How about you put on your new party hat," I said, "and we can go watch some more videos."

Lesson #11: *Embrace life's passages. Literally. Live in the moment. Even if that "moment" happens to stretch into three-and-a-half hours sitting on the cold bathroom floor waiting for a "special friend."*

And remind yourself, frequently, that you know almost no *40-year-olds who are still in diapers.*

12

Embrace Your Differences

Damn the torpedoes. Full speed ahead.

There are all sorts of different types of people in this world—those who, in the presence of bees, leap and gyrate around like Tina Turner, hysterically waving their arms and screaming, "*BEE! OH MY GOD! BEE*!" And those who just stand there quietly. The Over-reactor, and the Under-reactor.

I'm not going to say that I'm an Over-reactor—WHERE IN THE *HELL* DID YOU GET THAT IDEA?! I'VE JUST ABOUT HAD IT WITH YOUR *LOUSY ACCUSATIONS*—or that my husband is an Under- reactor—"Uh, honey? The house is on fire. You probably ought to amble on outside"

But still.

Men and women are so grossly unlike that, it's no wonder, entire sections of bookstores are devoted to tips on harmonious co-existence between the genders.

John Gray, best-selling author of *Men Are from Mars, Women Are from Venus*, points out, insightfully, that, basically, men and women are different. Wow. And shoes go on the feet. Thanks, John. Keen, cutting-edge observations like that have truly changed my life.

Kurt Vonnegut wrote, "Men are jerks, women are psychotics."

This theory might be a little closer. And it might explain why, for instance, my friend Janelle—a sweet, gentle and loving person, yes, but one who'd been up with a newborn most of the night—once hurled an omelette pan through a window as her husband left to play golf.

I've never hurled an omelette pan. I'd like to think that this is due to the fact that I have greater self-restraint. That I'm more centered, have more self-control, a broader perspective.

But it may have something to do with the fact that I don't actually *own* an omelette pan.

Instead of displacing cookware we don't have, my husband and I attempt to civilly work out our differences. For instance, I tell him that he's a "STUPID, ROTTEN IDIOT WITH MITE DUNG FOR BRAINS." But I say it in a nice way.

Also, we civilly twist each other's words into entirely different meanings. We lace our civil sparring with phrases like, "you *always* this, you *never* that." We generously provide each other with the always-popular Silent Treatment. We use Guilt whenever possible.

In other words, we've embraced our differences. We've learned to function as a team. You know, sort of how the Israelis and Palestinians are a team.

For instance, just this morning, he made toast while I buttered it, dressed the kids, answered a series of pointed Sam Donaldson-like questions regarding the nature of nasal discharge—"But where does it COME from?! Why is it green?! Is my brain green?!"—fed the kids, fed the dogs, cleaned the floors, and took out the trash.

Obviously, we've learned to embrace our differences. For instance, I do everything and he does squat. Yin and yang. I converse and extrapolate, examining, reexamining, and reexamining again all topics. He does silence and *Cliff's Notes*. He likes cake, I like frosting.

By accepting these differences, we've become highly compatible. Sort of like Bill Clinton and Ken Starr. Latrell Sprewell and P. J. Carlesimo. Tyson and Holyfield. Abbott and Costello. We've learned that the key to any thriving relationship, short of separate residences, is to love and understand one another.

And to keep omelette pans out of the house.

Lesson #12: *Different strokes for different folks.*

There are vast differences between all people, not just men and women. For instance, whenever I get a nasty letter from someone in response to a marvelously entertaining column I've written and I tell my dad about the letter, his standard response is, "It takes all kinds." Of course, this also happens to be his response to the question, "How are you?" and "What's the weather like there?"

"It takes all kinds, Linds," he says.

Men and women, young and old, smart and stupid, charming and obnoxious, chatty or silent—our differences make life so much more interesting! So much more exciting! So much more . . . infuriating!

13

Embrace Pain

Francis Thompson once wrote, "For we are born in other's pain, and perish in our own." An upbeat, party guy if ever there was one.

But it's true. Life is full of pain. Even without underwire bras.

If nothing else, I'm an optimist. As testimony to this fact, I once took a Lamaze class.

"The key to a more manageable childbirth," I read in some of the class materials, "is in knowing how to breathe."

I suppose there's some truth to that. I suppose that breathing makes childbirth more manageable if, say, you consider the alternative—*not* breathing. Which would make you *dead* and, as such, you might find childbirth, just a hunch, more difficult.

But still. In my experience, I've found that breathing, while commendable, is only a small part of the childbirth process. The larger part involving loud and tasteless profanity, grunting, sweating, and threats to the nursing staff that, when this is over, you will find out where each and every one of them lives.

Not to mention the loving and intimate exchanges with your husband, who is billing himself as the "labor coach," an overpaid job if ever there was one.

"*Breathe, Lindsey!*" he said encouragingly, during the labor and delivery of our first child.

"*Shut up, you hunk of stinkin' dog excrement!*" I answered tenderly, looking for something to throw at him.

But don't take my word for it. Basically, there are three schools of thought when it comes to childbirth:

1. Those who've never gone through it, or who haven't gone through it anytime recently, focus on relaxation and breathing, pillows, music, ice chips.

2. Those who've been through it focus on Major Drugs.

3. Those who believe the experience is nothing if not cinematic opt to videotape the whole thing.

Not that I'm advocating the use of Major Drugs. There are all sorts of people who experience wonderful, magical childbirths, and do so without the use of drugs. It's just that, personally, I've never met any of them.

So why, you ask, are we even taking a brush-up Lamaze class? Is it the fun of gathering together with other uncomfortable, waddling, and otherwise anxious pregnant people? The really gross videos of the birth process? Complete with graphic close-ups of grunting, sweating women whose mere facial expressions are enough to destabilize entire nations?

No.

It's optimism.

Okay, and fear.

Okay, okay, it's fear and desperation.

Because to be fair, breathing *did* help me during the early stage of my first childbirth—that extraordinary time when you walk around the hospital in a gown with your butt exposed to the world, in order to "keep things moving." As if there's a choice.

Breathing also helped me during *active* labor—that special time when mascara is smeared all over your face, your hair is in your eyes and, when you catch a glimpse of yourself in the bathroom mirror, you look like a deranged mental patient.

Breathing even helped me when a hospital maintenance person insisted—according to *her* schedule—on mopping my labor room floor. When I asked her to not mop my floor, pointing out that the floor was *just fine*, and rotated my head 360 degrees around on my neck to show that I meant business, she continued to mop the floor.

Fortunately, all this breathing and mopping of floors leads, eventually, to *delivery*—that special, indescribable time in life when you finally discover how loud you can really shout.

With the possible exception of hemorrhoids, after delivery, all is right with the world. You lie in bed while others take care of you, bringing you food and flowers, cleaning the room, changing the sheets.

And resting in your arms is this adorable, precious, bundled-up Miracle, who you'll love and cherish for the rest of your life—even when he or she gets small, green peas stuck in his nose, learns to drink water out of the dog's water dish, draws on the living room wall, throws tantrums, and sticks small objects into the electrical outlets—okay, keep breathing, keep breathing.

Lesson #13: *Whoever said, "No pain, no gain," was some sort of deranged psychopath. Of course there can be gain without pain—consider the effects of Häagen Dazs, for instance.*

Nonetheless, pain can be useful. It gets our attention. Makes us sit up and take notice. Helps us make changes in our lives. Sharpens our focus. Gives us the courage to use loud and vulgar profanity with perfectly nice health care providers.

PART III

ALTER YOUR EXPECTATIONS

Also, lower them.

Big time.

It's not that we should settle for the dregs in life; we should all have enormous success, harmonious relationships, stimulating and fulfilling jobs, rich friendships, and expensive and excessive material goods. We should have all these things. It's just that it's dangerous to expect them.

Believe me, you're setting yourself up for disaster.

For instance, I just learned about a New Jersey woman who rammed her car into her neighbor's house, then barricaded herself in her home for a twenty-hour standoff with police, all because her neighbor's sprinkler was making a puddle in her yard.

What? She expected life to be puddle-free?

I also heard about the eight Connecticut legislators who attended a reception sponsored by lobbyists for the Connecticut

Food Association. The politicians expected to be wined and dined. Instead they got severe enough diarrhea and stomach cramps that it made the news.

Oh sure, it's okay to *want* things to go a certain way. It's okay to *want* to go through life diarrhea and cramp-free. But is it reasonable? Well, I suppose that depends on how much you like burritos.

Burritos not withstanding, we don't always get what we want.

For instance, a long time ago, I wanted to be head cheerleader. When I didn't become head cheerleader I had to accept it, learn to live with it, move on.

Never mind that my way of living with it involved repeatedly egging the head cheerleader's house, and throwing rocks at her car, and making out with her boyfriend at parties.

Alter your expectations. Really. Because life has a funny way of shifting and bouncing around. Just when you think you know exactly what to expect, BOOM. Surprise! You don't. Rigidly clinging to hard and fast expectations is a recipe for disaster.

Let me show you the ways.

14

Expect Turbulence

Airplane travel with a young child is symbolic, in so many ways, of Life. It's turbulent. Quite aside from any atmospheric conditions.

Don't you go to weddings and relish the beauty, the magic of it? Everyone's faces shiny and bright, beautiful floral arrangements, cake, dancing, the wonderful celebration of true love? Don't you just sit there and think, "I'll give this two years, three years tops. These nutty kids don't have a clue what's down the road."

Work can be turbulent. One day you feel you're on the road to something, the next you can't believe you didn't go to business school. Plus, the office busy-bodies are starting to leave more and more indignant notes on the company 'fridge regarding the inappropriate consumption of someone's stupid yogurt, a meeting about downsizing lasts too long, and it's beautiful outside.

Flying with my son reminds me of an incident that occurred years ago, when I attended a big Los Angeles opening of a major play. During a crucial, poignant, dramatic moment in the standing-room-only theater, as the audience watched silently, intensely, I developed a massive case of giggles.

I couldn't help it.

I covered my face with my hands, concentrated on bad things—death, disease, control top panty hose—but the harder I tried to stifle myself, the more knee-slapping hysterical I became. The point is, you can't imagine the angry, evil looks I got.

Unless, of course, you have a child who you take on airplanes. In that case, you can *definitely* imagine the nasty looks.

It's irritating. Like, right, flying is such a pleasurable experience—what with the expansive leg room, the comfy seats, the gourmet meals—that my child and I, just by our mere presence, are ruining everybody's delirious fun?

Which is why I often take out my frustration on all the childless travelers, idiots nestled all snug in their seats and firing blistering looks my way, by whacking them upside the head with a free-swinging diaper bag.

"Oopsie-daisy," I say. "Did that silly diaper bag get you?" *Whack.*

And do they think it's *fun* trying to ram a *three-foot-long* baby stroller into a *two-foot-long* overhead compartment? Especially when the compartments are already filled with junk from people who were supposed to let parents with small children board first?

No, me either. Which is why I don't intervene when my youngster plays four solid hours of peek-a-boo over the seat with them. Or kicks the seat in front of us until the passenger needs back surgery.

And do they think it's *fun* trying to change a poopy diaper in one of those airline bathrooms?

No, me neither. Which is why I always have very stern

talks with my kid, before boarding all flights, about the absolute importance of avoiding mid-flight poops. "Remember, Mommy doesn't like to fly in the first place," I explain. "Mommy doesn't want to take her seat belt off, and stand in the nice little bathroom juggling Pampers, Baby Wipes, and poopy diapers, while the nice Captain is making the plane go bouncedy, bouncedy, bouncedy."

And do they think it's *fun* being thrown up on?

No, me either. Which is why I make a point of traveling with my husband. Especially after the time my son consumed approximately his own body weight in mini Ritz Bits, allowed his internal organs to process them for a while, then spewed the unsavory by-product all over my husband. Thank goodness that the highly trained flight attendants pulled together—a brilliant cadre of problem-solvers—by locating, then giving, my husband three, you count 'em, cocktail napkins.

And do they think it's *fun* doing magic tricks with graham crackers for hours on end, singing the "Itsy-Bitsy Spider," and making up stories to coincide with the pictures on the flight safety card?

"Oh look, honey! It must be Halloween! All the silly people are putting masks over their faces! And now they're all going down a great, big slide! Uh-oh! The plane must have had a boo-boo!"

Which is why, on our last flight, we figured out a delightful way to break up the monotony, while simultaneously responding to the creep who kept giving us dirty looks. We realized that a juice box can be converted into the sort of device that can douse people up to seven feet away.

Lesson #14: *Even if you expect the unexpected, you still won't get what you expect in life. Count on it. It's part of the in-flight turbulence plan. Just remember, short of Ritz Bits barf, that which does not kill you only makes you stronger.*

15

Expect a Lot of Baloney

Full of it. People, by and large, are full of it.

This was never clearer to me than when I set out to buy my first piece of Serious (read: expensive) Art. Gallery owners would say things like this: "Look at this! It's very Important Work! The Tension! The Contradiction! It's Controlled. Yet . . . Free."

"Yup," I used to add, surprised at how much I sounded like Gomer Pyle. "And it sure is a purty picher!"

But these days, some three trillion galleries later, I might answer, "Why, yes. It Creates, almost Nurtures, a sense of Confusion, yet Clarity. In such. A Youthful. Blossoming. Mocking Way."

The art aficionados love that kind of crud. Especially if you have a goatee. Which I do. But enough about my electrolysis problems. The point is, that sort of banter gets you right into the Club of Galleries and Openings and Pretension and Bucks and Baloney.

Case in point: an acquaintance of mine, someone with a lot of money and accompanying attitude, says he only buys "investment-quality" art, which to my mind, is about the same as saying, "Hi, I'm an ostentatious, over-inflated wind-bag with lots of money! But not necessarily taste! Go figure!"

So it gave me tremendous comfort when I recently read that 99 percent of the art bought in the United States each year doesn't appreciate, that it's not an "investment" at all, and that you should buy—GULP—what you *like*.

Fine. No problemo. Except that, it's hard to find things to like.

In New York, for example, there's an exhibition of three-and-a-half tons of cow bones, all shipped from Brazil, packed into a pool-like structure made up of 60,000 candles, weighing another two tons, and, naturally, shipped from Brazil.

In Los Angeles, I saw an exhibit of a square room with bare white walls and floor, and one light bulb. It was a GE light bulb, in case that means something Significant, and the exhibit was called "Community" or "Immunity" or "Impunity."

A bare room with one light bulb? Bonus. I already had that piece in my collection.

The more traditional galleries—ones with paintings of ladies under pastel-colored umbrellas—seem to have cornered the market on frames that are so busy, so ornate, so dizzying that, just by staring, you can develop vertigo.

At a gallery in Carmel, California, for example, where it is entirely possible that many art dealers moonlight as used car salesmen, I watched a young couple stare at one of those waves-crashing-on-rocks-with-seagulls-at-sunset paintings. Ever seen The Discovery Channel? The dealer was like a hungry lion closing in on a pair of unsuspecting gazelles. He attempted to disable and disorient them by getting a light show going with the dimmer switch.

"It's really an Important piece," he told them.

Surprisingly, though, those folks had discerning tastes.

"Do you have anything. . . ," the man ventured, "Do you have anything with . . . sea lions?"

I'm not making that up. But who could blame him? You spend a fortune on a painting, you'd think that the least you should get is a marine mammal or two.

Besides the dimmer-switch thing, there are a couple of other tricks gallery owners pull. For instance, they'll stand behind you while you're looking at a painting, nod approvingly, and say, "You must be an artist."

It got me the first time. About being an artist. I said, "Well-no." Then I thought about it and added, "But I have always had a keen sense of color and design, and, come to think about it, I'm highly creative."

And then they ask, "Are you a collector?" Avoid responding, "of what." Because what those gallery folks mean by that question is: "Are you anyone, or are you merely some sort of bacterial infection?"

So I say, "Ah, yes, I am a Collector, but alas, I have no Matisse."

Of course, in some circles Matisse would be majorly unhip. The art world's a smorgasbord, and people seem to get polarized on what they think is good. It's a have-to-take-sides kind of thing. You're either Rush Limbaugh or Howard Stern.

So these days, I display both avant-garde and traditional art books on my coffee table to announce my eclectic but hip taste. And occasionally I attend an Opening, where I can be heard exclaiming, "What Freedom, what Constraint! What use of Color, what use of Light! What Traditional Creativity, offset by such Unconventional Unimagination!"

It's like calling really old, useless junk "vintage." It gives it another dimension. But mostly, it's a whole lot of baloney.

Lesson #15: *People everywhere are full of baloney. Expect it. At parties, at work, at art galleries. The best way to disarm such people is to be free of all baloney. For instance, in an art gallery, if a dealer asks you if you're interested in a particular $20,000 painting, say, "CHRIST! Are you nuts? I couldn't even make my Hyundai payment last month! No, siree, I'm just in here killin' some time 'til the bus gets here. Then I'm off to Costco for a 48-pack of two-ply!"*

16

Expect Simple Pleasures

Lots of folks are looking for simplication in their lives. Fine. European vacations are simple. Porsches are simple. Diamonds and emeralds are simple. I'm totally into this Simplification trend. This make-life-easier business, this go-back-to-our-roots stuff.

But I'm going to keep my subscription to *Travel and Leisure*. And I'll probably keep the computer, the cell phone, and the microwave. Also, I don't want to grow my own vegetables, too much work. I don't want to sew my own clothes, too much work. I don't want to bake homemade bread, too much work.

Basically, the only thing I'm going to keep simple is—my parties. No torches, no swing bands, no catered meals. Just good, simple conversation:

"So-ooo . . . "

"Soooo-oooo . . . "

"Sooo, uh, yeah. . . ."

There are many key elements to planning a simple yet successful party. First, determine a (simple) theme. A formal Great Gatsby black-tie dinner, perhaps. Or a casual Ecuadorian potluck. Themes give guests a common bond, a sense of shared destiny, and possible conversation topics.

I kept a simple theme for my son's first birthday party, I sadly recall. It was sort of a Vomit Theme. He was sick, in his crib, and missed the entire occasion. Folks spent several hours discussing such provocative party talk as, "Do you suppose he's contagious?" and "I remember once when I got really sick at a party. . . ."

Keep decorations simple. Because the masses of crepe paper? All the balloons? They'll fall down before anyone gets there.

Limit the party to one room of the house. The simplest way to keep people from overflowing into other rooms is to have one of your dogs produce remarkably explosive diarrhea all over the living room rug five minutes prior to party time. Think of all the fun to be had as guests discuss: their own harrowing experiences with carpet stains and the downside of indoor pets.

Keep the party food simple by making several quiches, all of which completely flop. Think sludge in a pie pan. Guests can mingle with each other discussing topics such as: "We ate before we came," and "Well, you know, quiches are really hard to make, what with having to actually crack those doggone eggs and all."

A couple of summers ago, I threw a pool party. I kept it simple since we didn't actually have a pool. Guests gathered around a simply pleasurable four-foot plastic wading tub we'd put out on our deck, periodically dipping their hands into the water, and saying, "Geez, this IS the good life!" Your friends will have *plenty* to talk about. Such as whether or not the house is air-conditioned.

All you really need is fresh air, good-hearted souls, a sense of fun, and a big bag of snack mix.

Halloween costume party? Snack mix in a jack-o-lantern. Formal Christmas dinner? Snack mix in a green and red dish. Polynesian luau? Snack mix in a coconut.

People *love* snack mix. They eat a lot of it, and they say things like, "Wow, this is really good snack mix" or "I shouldn't have eaten so much snack mix" or "What a simple, lovely pleasure in life—snack mix!"

Simple themes and simple food alone, however, aren't enough to make a party swing. Another key element of successful party-giving, then, is the guest list. Keep it simple. Invite people who you think might argue a lot. It reduces the pressure on the other folks to keep the conversation going.

For instance, once I hosted a dinner for a couple with two screaming toddlers, another couple with no kids, a single man with a bad headache, an exchange student who spoke no English, a vegan, a carnivore, four omnivores, and a woman who claimed to be a reptile in a previous life.

Lesson #16: *We should all expect simple pleasures—even if they are highly complicated. The simple pleasure of a beach sunset, for instance, pretty much involves a travel agent, airfare to Hawaii, and hotel reservations. The simple pleasure of a child's smile of glee on Christmas morning involves nine months of pregnancy, morning sickness, and delivery, for the love of God, as well as having to actually find a parking space at the mall to buy the %&#*! presents for the little brat. Ah, simplicity. It's not always what you expect.*

17

Expect the Unexpected

"Romance" is a relative term. What's romantic to one person is disposable razor blades to another.

I'm talking about a friend who received from her husband, on the always-sacred Valentine's Day, a package of disposable razor blades.

Oh sure, it was a *whole pack* of them, and they'd never been used by anyone else or anything, and they were a nice shade of blue, like the color of her eyes, which he may have specifically had in mind. But I doubt it.

My friend Cathy received a really "romantic" pair of gray down slippers that made her feet look the approximate size of Buicks.

And years ago, when my husband planned our "romantic" honeymoon, we wound up on a remote island in Fiji—just the two of us, and a truly revolting number of sea snakes. And lizards. Even now, so many years later, I just fire up with venom when I think about those blasted lizards parading across our hut's ceiling, periodically losing their footing and sky-diving onto my pillow where, sometimes, my actual face was located.

The point is, in Life and in Romance, we should expect the unexpected.

To that end, a bunch of wackos have been pushing an annual "Romance Awareness Month." It is billed as a "public-service program" because, basically, *anyone* can call *anything* a public-service program. In fact, this book is a public-service program, so send your donations to me, instead of the Red Cross. The goal of Romance Awareness Month, ostensibly, is to educate couples about the value of romance as an important part of daily living.

I don't know about you, but romance is a HUGE part of my daily living. In fact, recently I experienced one particularly dynamic *sexually charged* moment, when my husband came downstairs wearing dark socks with his Nikes. I felt like an *ANIMAL!*

But I digress.

Optimistic organizers of Romance Awareness Month hope to: (1) make money while encouraging couples to keep the sizzle in their relationship by celebrating romance; (2) make money while informing couples that individual personality styles determine how one perceives romance, and; (3) make money while offering couples suggestions for celebrating romance in unique, inexpensive ways.

Yes, for only $29.95 you can purchase a "*boxed* romantic adventure." What is romance, after all, if not "boxed?"

One such adventure is called "The French Rabbit." I have absolutely no idea why. I don't want to know. Nonetheless, using a series of "*intriguing cards*," which I can only guess have rabbits pictured all over them, you "*lead your partner on a pursuit of the mysterious and elusive French Rabbit.*"

Hello? Have I been missing something? Because frankly, this raises a number of questions, not the least of which is, what the hell is a *"French rabbit?"* How is it different from, say, an American rabbit, and why is it "elusive?" Also, in what way, exactly, is any of this romantic?

The kit includes seven cards and envelopes, a rabbit, rabbit cookie cutter, rabbit ears, a bow tie and "ultimately the exciting and surprise-filled treasure hunt will lead to a romantic rendezvous with you." God.

Another "boxed" romantic adventure is called "A Formal Affair," and includes five cards and envelopes, a hand-painted penguin, romantic music, two pillowcases, and recipes.

Okay, a penguin? A *hand-painted* penguin? Excuse me, but where are the drug-sniffing dogs when you need them?

There were a number of other really "romantic" suggestions in my media pack, including, but not limited to, sending your *"King or Queen"* an invitation to dinner that says, *"The presence of Your Royal Majesty is requested at a Feast of Admiration prepared in your honor."*

With dessert, you're supposed to present a scroll that begins, *"Hear Ye! Hear Ye! Take heed and listen to the wonderful attributes of Your Royal Majesty,"* and then list the attributes. Or maybe—and this is just my vampy, sensual spin on it—list what chores your spouse needs to do around the house.

Another suggestion involves writing: *"You Tarzan, me Jane. Let's swing tonight!"* on the bathroom mirror—WITH LIPSTICK!

Knock, knock. Anyone home? Who do you suppose is going to be cleaning that mirror?

Yet another suggestion proposes that you send a bottle of Tabasco sauce to your sweetie with a note that says, *"If you think this is hot, wait until you see me tonight!"*

Listen, if I defaced the bathroom with cosmetics, or mailed hot sauce, or started marching around the house saying, "Hear

Ye, Hear Ye!" I think it's safe to say that my husband's romantic, and entirely appropriate response, would be to immediately contact a highly trained therapist.

Lesson #17: *Life is full of surprises, unexpected twists and turns. Particularly when it comes to romance. For instance, my husband once planned a romantic rendezvous where his first topic of conversation was, namely, bunions. I can't tell you how much I wish I'd made that up.*

Oh sure, we can plan, wish for, even agonize over the way we think things ought to be. But there are certain elements beyond our control. Case in point, granulated foot tissue.

We can only hope that disposable razors, giant slippers, and LSD-inspired "boxed romances" aren't among them.

18

Don't Expect Miracles

"Menstrual Cramps: What They *Mean*—And What They *Say* About You!"

"Job Interviews: How the Right Nail Color Can Land the Job!!"

"Thighs: Firm and Thin—While You *Sleep!*"

"10 *Hot* Spots for Meeting the *Hot* Man of Your Dreams!"

"Exfoliation: How it Can Completely Change Your Life— *Our Experts Tell All!*"

"Entertaining: How to Throw a *Gourmet* Dinner For 30— in Just 15 *Minutes*! *For Under $5.00!*"

People expect so much. For instance, I just read a lengthy article on becoming organized. Of course, with all the time it took me to read the blasted article, I ran out of time to actually *do* anything organizational.

"Why don't you write more articles for women's magazines?" my friends always ask. ("How Asking Great Questions Can Help Burn Cellulite!!")

"There are so many women's magazines," they say. "We'd have thought that you'd want to write for one of them!"

Sorry, but I've never been all that comfortable with so many exclamation points!!! Besides, there are other—ethical—issues. For instance, what makes me an expert on how to: "Redecorate Your Living Room Using Items from Your Trash!"

Do I need to attend some sort of certification program before I pen, "Sexual Positions: Doing It in the Laundry Room—The Importance of Fabric Softener"?

Nonetheless, the editors of those magazines know what they're doing. Women buy them. I buy them. We expect miracles.

Perhaps it's total escapism for me—the fashions, the bodies, the faces, the articles. Perhaps it's a reprieve from Regular Life, from the daily grind, from news of interest rates and politics.

Because, come on: At the end of the day, when I'm too tired to move or think, much less seduce anything, what sheer entertainment value to read: "10 Ways to *Seduce* a Man Using Leftover Saran Wrap!"

For instance—TRUE STORY—I once saw a magazine article on seduction and one of its ten recommended ways to seduce a man was to "Draw a Beauty Mark on Your Face."

Uh, hello?

I got the wind knocked out of me when I read that, like someone just jumped on my belly. So I marched right into the bathroom and made black pencil marks all over my face.

Moments later, when my husband caught sight of me, when

I "seductively" opened the bathroom door looking like Pippi Longstocking, he responded in this sensual, animalistic, primal way. He said:

"God. You've been reading women's magazines!" ("Men Who Don't Respond to Black Pencil Marks on Your Face—And What It Says about Your Marriage!—and How You Can Fix It with One Tuna Casserole!!")

Maybe I should have consulted my horoscope. Maybe I read the wrong article. But the editors of those magazines know what they're doing. They know I'll flip a few pages and try, try again.

Lesson #18: *It's a good thing—at least for the magazine industry—that most of us are needy, empty, and deeply insecure. They know we're driven by the never-ending quest for easy, simple miracles. It's not enough to be a success at business, or a good parent, or a top athlete, or a gifted host, or a fashion plate, or a supermodel. We're programmed to believe that we need to be all of them.*

There it is! My BIG magazine idea!

"How to Be a Rich, Successful Mother Who Wins Triathlons while Preparing Gourmet Meals for High-Style Dinner Parties Held in Your Architectural Digest *Home—While Having Great Sex and Looking Fabulous!!"*

19

On the Road of Life, Expect Some Bad Trips

I recently took a bad trip.

Not that I stumbled and fell, or had an unpleasant experience with illegal narcotics. By "bad trip," I mean, simply, that I was in the car, for an extended period of time, with my family.

Let me define "extended period of time." It's the approximate amount of time it takes to start the engine and back out of the garage.

Don't get me wrong. I love my family. I'd do anything for them. Climb tall mountains, swim cold rivers, call them long-distance from a really great resort, maybe even send them a nice postcard.

Just don't strap me into the car with them, for an extended period of time.

"By most informed accounts, driving trips are one of America's favorite vacation choices," I read in an article from the *Washington Post*, proving, once again, that you can't believe everything you read in newspapers.

Case in point, I've also recently seen these headlines: "High-Tech Wedding Band Warns if Your Husband Is Fooling Around," and "Phone Sex Made Me Pregnant." But I digress.

Here are the article's pointers:

1. Build the trip around your interests and those of your family. Well, gee. You mean, find a rock quarry for my son? So he can chuck stones all day? Find a toxic waste site for my young daughter? So she can find the grossest thing possible to jam into her little mouth? Find a map store for my husband, or any set of complicated directions, preferably written in Korean? So he can stare blankly at paper for hours on end?

2. Buy or borrow a guidebook. A guidebook? *Just one*? Listen, we had guidebooks coming out of the hoo-ha. Cruel, taunting guidebooks listing all the wonderful restaurants, charming inns, and sophisticated shops full of highly breakable items where we won't be able to dine, sleep, or shop until our kids are, say, much older, or incarcerated.

3. Shun the interstates. Fine. They're shunned already. For one thing, they don't have a bathroom every fifteen to twenty feet, which one needs when traveling with youngsters. Also, by sticking to the beautiful and scenic back roads, the trip becomes far more interesting. And here I'm thinking about the time when everyone got really carsick and started vomiting.

4. Choose interesting lodgings, and make reservations in advance. "*Interesting*," it should be noted, is a term open to broad interpretation. We stayed at a motel, once, where the air conditioning unit actually fell out of the wall in the middle of the night. That was interesting. On another occasion, a highly popular national holiday during which everyone, apparently, had decided

to travel, we skipped the oh-so-crucial "making reservations" part. Eight hours from home without a "Vacancy" sign in sight, we had quite an "interesting" drive back to our house.

5. Limit the number of miles you cover daily. *Huh?* Between bathroom stops, lunch stops, and little breaks to "get out and stretch our legs," it was 7 p.m. by the time my family and I actually drove out of town limits.

6. Pack a picnic. Tums and Tylenol.

7. Use your imagination. "Almost any part of America is worth a look," the article states. This, simply, is a big freakin' lie. At approximately 8 p.m. on the same night we left town, for instance, now all of *22 miles* from our home—practically on another continent—we stopped for a photo op at a run-down gas station. It wasn't exactly the cover of *Travel and Leisure* magazine but, alas, it had become clear that we needed to talk to someone with expertise about the shortcomings of our radiator.

The gas station was closed, and the only guy we saw was a fellow "just passing through," on a nice driving trip with his family, lost, and asking for directions.

Lesson #19: *Whoever said, "Enjoy the journey, not just the destination," apparently has never been in a second-rate car, on a lengthy trip, with thirsty, hungry, and bored kids. Because clearly, sometimes the journey just ain't all that hot.*

Then again, sometimes it is. Especially when you learn to ease up a bit, roll with the punches, and dramatically lower your standards! In other words, alter your expectations. Then it can actually be sort of interesting. Sort of.

PART IV

LOOK ON THE BRIGHT SIDE

Once, I had to sit through nearly three hours of dragged-out pain and suffering. The bright side? Lots of people would've killed to have those front row seats of mine at *Cats*. So I didn't complain. That's the kind of person I am. I look on the bright side.

So, as I sat there in the dark, watching a guy in cat makeup pounce and meow around the stage, I counted my blessings. Did I have a headache? No. Did I have tuberculosis? No. Bronchitis? Again, no. Liver disease, inflammatory bowel, or ingrown toenails? No, no, and no.

You see, I was looking on the bright side.

Looking on the bright side is one of the most valuable skills we can develop. Right after making a lot of money. And learning how to exert mind-control over other people.

We can transform almost any negative situation into something that's good and positive. I say *almost any* because once, at a dinner party, despite my high-level of looking-on-the-bright-side training, I was miserable.

The dinner table discussion had turned, regrettably, to natural childbirth. Several individuals had gotten quite passionate about the fact that women who don't have "natural childbirth" are probably not, in fact, real women.

Try as I might to etch lovely patterns of mashed potato around my plate, I felt I needed to speak up.

"Uh, I'd like to define *un*-natural childbirth," I offered. "To me, unnatural childbirth is that in which the infant is born through one's ear canal."

The bright side of that remark—in addition to my own personal satisfaction—was that several of the individuals looked as if, right then and there, they were in the throes of hard labor!

Naturally, of course.

Recently, when my young daughter spent an entire morning whining and fussing—the juice was in the wrong cup, her brother looked at her the wrong way, she hated the socks I put on her, the barometric pressure was off—I'd finally had it.

"Skyler!" I snapped. "Tell me one *good* thing about your morning!"

She was quiet for a moment, then she said, "Our dogs aren't dead?"

Uh . . . right. Okay. Pretty weird, but I'll take it. At least it's a step in the right direction.

20

Look on the Bright Side of Work

Monday.

People just hate Mondays. Dread them. Can't believe that their lives are so desperate and messed up that they've got to get up and go to work at that hell-hole one more day. The commute! The office politics! The incredible number of office idiots!

On the other hand, what about the long-distance calls to friends! Free memo pads! Handy high-speed Internet connection! Pens! Pencils!

What would we do without work?

Personally, I love professional challenge and stimulation. Which is why I always bring one of my dogs with me to the office so that I can spend most of my day—when I'm not having coffee, or lunch, or calling long-distance friends—trying to remove shedded pet hair from my file folders.

As a professional writer, you see, the crux of my time is involved in tapping into my creative, inventive self, observing and becoming one with the world around me.

In other words, I waste a lot of time.

"Why do you do what you do?" people always ask me. "Why did you become a writer? How can you stand to be on perpetual deadline?"

It's rather simple. For years I'd felt a burning in my soul, an itch, an inner voice screaming to be heard, if you will, a need to reach out and touch the world in a way the world had never been touched.

Also, I didn't want to go to business school.

So I figured, what they hey, I'll become a writer. I'll be able to justify my mood swings and attribute all my numerous short-comings to the fact that I'm a brooding artiste. All without the requirement of having to wear pantyhose and pumps.

Before I became a writer, I held a number of real awful jobs. The bright side of that? Pretty much nothing!! Oh sure, I learned how to be creative when I worked as a waitress. For instance, if I had to carry a tray of six margaritas all the way across the restaurant, and the margaritas were all filled right to the brim, what did I do? Well, I slurped a little out of each glass, of course. So you see, also, I learned about problem-solving.

Not only did the margaritas not spill en route to the table, but also I felt a whole lot jollier about the work I was doing.

Right after college, I worked in the U.S. Senate as a legis-lative aide. I worked really long hours, for really little money, and was constantly being thrown into situations where I felt— and acted—like an idiot. The upside? Uh . . . well, that would be . . . uh . . . oh yeah! I learned how to survive looking and sound-ing and feeling like an idiot. A skill that would serve me well later in life.

Also, I worked in the U.S. State Department where—bright side—I had the unique opportunity to witness how our govern-ment actually functions. Let me just say this about that. It took nearly six months to go through the "proper channels" to get a lamp in my office. But hey! I got it, didn't I? Someone finally saw the light.

Some people think that, without work, life would be a lot more fun, a lot more fulfilling. Well, duh. I mean, that's dumb. We should try to find the bright side of work. As British author Jerome K. Jerome once said, "I like work; it fascinates me. I can sit and look at it for hours. I love to keep it by me; the idea of getting rid of it nearly breaks my heart."

Lesson #20: *As human beings, we just LOVE to complain. Work helps us do that by giving us all sorts of things we can bitch about — unreasonable bosses, back-stabbing-busy-body coworkers, lousy commutes, inadequate pay and vacation time, pointless meetings, stupid memos, and restrictive dress codes.*

Also, we get money! And for some of us, a little quality downtime with our dogs.

21

Look on the Bright Side of Meetings

Donuts! Coffee! A refreshing nap, perhaps?

I love meetings.

To me, meetings are just the ticket when I need a vacation, but can't afford a trip to the Poconos—when I don't feel like working, but can't take time off.

"Go to a meeting!" I always tell my burned-out friends. "Keep score while others bicker over petty issues, enjoy some lovely refreshments, write letters, plan a party. Just make sure that you rub your eyes wearily, from time to time, and lean back in your chair pensively once in a while, and tap your pencil eraser on the table intensely, now and then, as if you're about to produce some genius idea."

Most people don't like to admit this.

They like to believe that meetings are such hard work that you have to keep replenishing your bodily fluids, which is why there's always a pitcher of water on the table.

Which is unfortunate because—true story—once I knocked over my glass of water during a particularly intense meeting, and the water spread like some kind of giant science-fiction amoeba. A lot of dark suits were scrambling to save their papers from the flood damage.

"Let's not cry over spilled water," I offered in an effort to look on the bright side.

You can't believe the looks I got. Fortunately, they were mostly from the sort of people who were always writing superfluous memos with a lot of run-on sentences, and taking reports home on weekends, so I shrugged it off.

Obviously, they'd never worked in the State Department, which is where I first learned about meeting fun.

For one thing, nothing was ever accomplished. Which may have had something to do with the fact that weekly State Department staff meetings consisted of approximately 475 people, all of whom were deathly afraid of missing *any* opportunity to brown-nose with an assistant-to-the-assistant-to-the-assistant deputy secretary of state.

"What did you learn today?" I once asked my colleague after our weekly staff meeting.

"That Mavis has really gross, yellow toenails," he said.

He was referring to another staff member, Mavis, whose name has been changed to protect me from being sued for revealing government secrets.

Yes, Mavis often wore open-toed shoes, thereby giving us something to stare at, and be entertained by, during meetings.

And once, after a press conference, which is nothing more than a meeting with reporters present to record all the idiotic things that are said, I asked this guy the same question:

"What did you learn at the press conference?"

"That Kate has really bad body odor," he said, referring to another colleague of ours, whose name has been changed because I think she's at the CIA now. Kate used to work out at lunch, but not shower, then squeeze into crowded press conferences leaving everyone grimacing and looking around for the offender.

"I think you're exaggerating," my husband said. "All meetings aren't that bad. In fact, a lot of meetings are useful, productive, and informative."

What a kidder.

I mean, a bright guy by all standardized testing methods, my husband suffers from this idealistic, but delusional notion, that meetings should follow an agenda. That only those people who will directly contribute to, or significantly benefit from, the stated agenda should attend. That the discussion should stay focused, decisions made, and tasks accomplished.

He's such a pessimist.

"How was your big meeting with Ray?" I asked him last week after he met with the chief financial officer at a major corporation.

"Terrible. He ate donuts, drank coffee, then went to sleep," he said. "Once I looked over at him and his eyes were rolling back into his head."

Damn! I missed all that?!

Lesson #21: *Everyone is always telling you to slow down, am I right? To relax, take a load off. Meetings provide that rare opportunity. Do a little deep breathing, chant a mantra. If you're called upon to say something, simply respond, "You know? I can't help thinking that we need to have more reliable data on this one,* *folks." This statement works in every situation. Then relax your neck and shoulders and dream of someplace with lots of sand and sunshine.*

22

Look on the Bright Side of Parenting

I don't want to brag or anything, but I have to be honest. I'm an incredible parent.

Of all the strong moral values I hope to instill in my toddler as he develops and matures into an adult—a sense of right and wrong, kindness toward others, generosity, and an enthusiasm and embracement of life—I've already managed, thank you very much, to instill one of the most important ones.

The ability to face the myriad of evils that awaits kids these days—drugs, alcohol, sex and violence—and to *Just Say No.*

Literally. The kids says it all the time. Pretty much non-stop. No, no, no, no. And he isn't even two years old!

"Let's go take a bath, honey," I recently said to him.

"No!"

"Do you want to wear the red shirt today?"

"NO!"

"Would you like to have your very own pony, a hundred puppies, several new toys and a souped-up Maserati with extra horse power and custom leather seats?"

"NO!"

"Okay, do you want to go to the park, and on the swings AND the slide, then feed the ducks, while simultaneously eating all the graham crackers and ice cream you can shovel in, then roll around in the mud, and get really, really dirty?"

"NO!!"

Clearly I've done my job well.

And the other Saturday morning when he was just beginning to stir, as my husband and I listened expectantly to the baby monitor for his usual chatty garblings and cooings, what we heard instead was U.S. Gen. George S. Patton.

"NO, NO, NO, NO, NO!"

Bless his heart. The little dear was starting his day with such impressive strength of conviction, such unyielding principles.

It was one of those magical moments in parenting, in fact, when you clench your jaw, because you know that you're in for yet another, and certainly not the last, roller-coaster ride.

Hey, at least we're past the stage when he was making loud, and remarkably accurate, donkey noises at perfect strangers in the supermarket.

"He's saying 'no!' and becoming obstinate?" my child-psychologist friend asked gleefully. "Congratulations! That's wonderful! I'm so happy for you! He's showing a positive sign of growth!"

A sign of growth? And I suppose bringing the car home late, armed robbery, and hijacking would be other signs?

"No, no, no, no, no," she said. God. It was contagious. Some sort of viral thing. "Your toddler has reached that exciting time in his development when he's just starting to understand that he's a separate person from you and, as such, is trying to test and express that awareness by initiating actions all by his own."

"In other words, the peanut butter hair-and-scalp massages he gives himself while eating his sandwich are a GOOD thing?" I asked. "And when he takes all the dirt from the potted plants and carries it to the sofa, or tries to ram his toy vacuum cleaner into the dogs while they're sleeping, or takes the straw out of his juice box and dumps the entire tasty beverage all over himself— THESE ARE GOOD THINGS?! Signs of *growth*? Milestones I should be happily including in this year's Christmas letter?!"

"Exactly!" she said. "And remember to roll with it! His saying 'no' to you is an important part of the developmental stage which will, eventually, lead to his understanding of responsibility."

Hmmm.

"Honey," I said, later that day, as I rocked the little peanut butter-head to sleep, "Did you know that you're growing up, asserting yourself, and becoming responsible?"

He stirred as I lowered him into his crib, and without opening his eyes, he muttered, "No."

Lesson #22: *As adults, we regress in one important way. We forget how to say "no." We say "yes" to everything and everybody, at work, at home, with friends, with family. We're exhausted, our lives are out of balance, we have no time for ourselves, and we're making Tylenol and Tums a steady part of our daily diet.*

Fortunately, parenting helps turn us from "yes" people, into "no" people. "Lindsey? We need you on our committee . . . " "No way! CAN'T YOU SEE THAT I'M BUSY?!" "Lindsey? Could you do a radio interview?" "NO!" Shoot, once you get the hang of it, you can't believe how fun and liberating it is to just say "NO!" all the time.

23

Look on the Bright Side of Being Ignored

"It was fine."

"It was okay."

"It was fine, I guess."

Talk about a gabfest. These are the kinds of lively and descriptive observations one might hear from my husband in response to a movie, a trip around the world, a bungee jump off a collapsing bridge into shark-infested waters, triple bypass surgery performed by blind Boy Scouts on a sugar rush.

"It was okay."

It was okay?

What is this? English as a second language?

Or is it another one of those areas that falls into the vast category of differences between men and women? But hey. Think of the bright side. Bad communication between men and women has really helped me to start listening to myself. Particularly because, I may be the only one listening.

Actually, it's scary how many differences there are between men and women. When I was suffering from world-record, projectile-vomiting morning sickness and had to be hospitalized and put on I.V. fluids, I still kept functioning, doing my job, holding my life together.

Conversely, when my husband got a cold recently, some killer virus which actually caused him to SNEEZE *TWICE*, he went to bed for *FOURTEEN HOURS*, all the time grunting and groaning like he was trying to pass a kidney stone.

Men and women are different. Women communicate; men go through the mail.

"So then I was diagnosed with inoperable cancer, and the car was impounded, and the house was burning down..."

"Wow! Did you see this free offer? If you get your car washed ten times, you get the next one free. There's a coupon right here in the mail..."

The bright side? *Someone* has to go through the mail.

I know what you're thinking. That some women talk too much. I disagree. Now let me finish what I was saying. But it's not that we talk too much, it's that we *hash*.

"Hashing" is not about illegal drugs, or chopped up meat and vegetables in a skillet.

To "hash": Today we are hashing; tomorrow we shall hash; in all my life I have hashed often. To "hash" is to take a topic, any topic that merits hashing, chop it, dice it, flip it, then come at it from another angle.

Ask me about a movie.

Not only will I discuss the plot, characters, scenery, soundtrack, special effects, dialogue, *and* all the people I saw in the bathroom, but also I'll be able to tell you what they were wearing, and what they were saying. I'll tell you what the people behind me in the popcorn line were arguing about, and I'll have several additional comments about the shape, size, and quality of Mel Gibson's butt.

I am woman, hear me bore.

In my defense, I've tried to meet my husband halfway on this conversational abyss. I've discussed the 49ers' strengths and the Lakers' weaknesses while guzzling a can of light beer and, periodically, adjusting the crotch of my pants.

In his defense, he's trying. I think he realized that our relationship might be more interesting if, say, we conversed about something other than the grocery list.

"Honey," I said as part of our nightly language session, "How's that book you're reading?"

"Okay, good, okay," he said. Whoa. Can this bad boy filibuster, or what?

"Well, is it a book I might enjoy?"

"Maybe. Maybe not. It's okay, I guess."

And the other day I caught my husband reading a book by Emily Post on how to make conversation. At dinner, then, he said: "On business, or is this visit purely pleasure?"

It gets weirder. When I was sitting around with some female friends a couple of weeks ago, he burst into the room, hysterically blurting out, "Fine, fine, all right, fine. It's a lovely day for a parade, isn't it?"

There's more. Last weekend, when we were at the movies, he kept turning to perfect strangers and saying, "It was *so* good of you to make it! We're just *delighted* to have you here! Make yourself at home! Can I get you a soda or some popcorn?"

I was frightened.

"How does it make you *feel*?" he asked me the other day as I was reading a book. "Does it awaken memories of your childhood? Do you respond to it on some deep, emotional level? Does it raise questions or self-doubt about who you are as a person?"

For God's sake. I was glancing at a lousy cookbook.

Now, every morning, he wakes up, wants to chat about the weather, including details about humidity and barometric pressure, and about toast and orange juice, sometimes even reading out loud the *ingredients label* on the back of the cereal box.

Frankly, I miss the old days, our special times together— me babbling on and on about absolutely anything that flittered into my head, with him sitting quietly through it all.

Lesson #23: *The bright side of being ignored is that, in turn, you don't have to listen to anyone else's really boring talk. You can have all the free air time you want! You don't have to take turns!*

So, before you complain too much about your life and its supposed inadequacies, about the way no one listens to you, pause. Ask yourself hard questions like: Do I really want to encourage periodic updates of barometric anomalies?

24

Look on the Bright Side of Long, Protracted Marriages

There are a number of key anniversaries to celebrate during early November—the first insect electrocutor was patented in 1910; the Exotic Dancers League of America formed in 1963; artificial snow was invented in 1946; and I was married in 1986.

"More than a decade?" I said to my husband. "Can you believe we've been married more than a decade?"

"No," he said. "In fact, it seems like much, much longer."

Mr. Stand-up! Mr. Comedy! What jocular, all-out, knee-slapping fun marriage can be! Just think—without marriage how could we ever find ourselves in that special position of having to say to another human being, *"For the love of God*, would you PLEASE stop clipping your nails at the dinner table?!"

Without marriage, how could we ever completely satisfy our Basic Human Need for back-seat driving?

Without marriage, how could we ever use that all-time favorite line, "I WISH YOU'D TRY TO UNDERSTAND MY POINT OF VIEW!"

And without long protracted marriages, how would any of us ever achieve extreme, mind-deadening, off-the-charts boredom.

I'm kidding. But not entirely.

Perhaps I should've known that something was *seriously wrong* with my future spouse many years ago on the 4th of July. We were walking along, on our way to see fireworks, and the guy put his hands in his pants.

Not to make a simple adjustment. No. Something much more serious was going on in those trousers, my friends, and clearly this fella was being driven by some primordial need. In fact, he was hopping and gyrating around like a pornographic Elvis knockoff, while parents of small children whisked their youngsters away.

It was a simple matter of a rogue mosquito, I was later told. Whatever.

Between that incident, and the time the Public Porn Star sat down at his piano to serenade me with a song from *West Side Story* ("*I feel pretty, oh so pretty, I feel pretty, and witty, and bright* . . ."), I knew that I'd found that one special person I could love, cherish, annoy, and criticize for the rest of my life.

"What do you suppose the secret to a long, good marriage is?" my young friend Karen once asked me.

"Frequent, highly charged affairs?" I offered.

The secret? I have absolutely no idea whatsoever, but putting the goddamn milk back in the fridge strikes me as a good place to start.

Also, I suspect that most marital disputes could be avoided if, for instance, the husband would say, approximately every three to four minutes, "Darling, you're the best thing that ever happened to me, and by the way, your hair looks sensational today!"

Short of that, it's important to remember four basic principles associated with long, protracted marriages:

1. Men and women are different. For instance, men are less demanding. They can be happy in a marriage as long as, say, the tires are rotated regularly. Women, on the other hand, want to discuss tire rotation and all of its ramifications—who did it, who was there, what they said, what that means, what impact it all might have on the relationship, and whether the tire rotation makes them look fat;

2. Marriage is no Michael Bolton song. Thank God. Who needs all that whining, squinting, and Rapunzel-like hair on a man;

3. Work on the relationship. In other words, freely and generously point out your spouse's faults whenever possible - the theory being, if you can't make the troublemaker behave the way you want, at least enjoy the fun of a really good fight, and;

4. Work as a team. For instance, if you happen to be a critical person, look for characteristics in your spouse that you can, for instance, criticize.

Lesson #24: *Look on the bright side of long, protracted marriage. Consider the alternative—you could be holed up in an apartment talking to cats. Shopping the Home Shopping Network. Reading about kinky sex in glossy magazines. Oh. You're doing all that anyway. Hmmm.*

Well, then. The point is, both individually and as couples, we have to learn how to accentuate the positive. For instance, when my husband leaves natty floss on the bathroom counters, I appreciate the fact that he hasn't left used Kleenex in, say, the fridge. Yet.

Also, you have to remember that there's a certain beauty to long-term relationships—and here I'm thinking, primarily, about the fact that you pretty much get to stop shaving all the time.

25

Life Isn't a Fairy Tale

It was a cold, rainy night, the wind pounded against the windows, the roof leaked, and the heater made sounds not unlike Pearl Harbor. The bright side? I snuggled up with my precious little children, in front of a crackling fire, homemade cookies hot out of the oven, and began reading them a few of the classic, heart-warming, age-old stories from my childhood:

"Rock-a-bye baby, on the tree top,

When the wind blows, the cradle will rock;

When the bough breaks, the cradle will fall,

Down will come baby, cradle, and all."

"*MOM!*" my son shouted. "The baby *fell*?"

"Oh, no, honey," I said, privately wondering what sort of psychopath had put a baby up in a tree. Surely, some agency should be called. Quickly, I flipped the page.

"Jack and Jill went up the hill

To fetch a pail of water;

Jack fell down and broke his crown,

And Jill came tumbling after."

"MOM!" my son shrieked, alarming his young sister. "Did the little girl get an 'ow'? Did she cry?"

"Oh honey, of course not! They were, uh, just hurrying down the hill so that they, uh, could have some *ice cream*." I grabbed another book. Something about animals. Happier topic. I pulled my dear children closer, cleared my voice, and read:

"Ladybird, ladybird,

Fly away home,

Your house is on fire

And your children are gone."

"*MOM*!" He was sobbing out of control now. "Is our house going to catch on fire, too?"

"No!"

"But what happened to the children?"

"The children? Oh. Well, the children went to the—uh—park, honey, where they—uh—ate a lot of *ice cream*. And *candy*. Why don't we find a happier story," I said, turning the pages.

"Three blind mice, see how they run!

They all run after the farmer's wife,

Who cut off their . . . "

Yikes. I jumped to the next chapter. Something about dogs. Perfect. I began:

"Old Mother Hubbard

Went to the cupboard

To fetch her poor dog a bone;

But when she came there

The cupboard was bare

And so the poor dog had none."

"MOM!" The dog was hungry!" my son was writhing on the floor, tears running down his face. "He just wants a Milkbone!"

"Sweetheart, sweetheart!" I said, drawing my young to me during this warm, magical Walton Family evening. "Here's the deal. Mother Hubbard ran out of Milkbones, it's true, but that's because she spent all her money on, uh, *ice cream*—and *toys*. So, instead of a boring ol' bone, the dog got a great big ice cream cone."

"Doggies don't eat ice cream."

"Huh? Oh. Right. Well, okay, this was *magic* ice cream, honey, it was *Milkbone* ice cream. Anyway, just listen. I'm sure it'll all turn out okay." I continued:

"She went to the baker's

To buy some bread;

But when she came back

The poor dog was dead."

"MOM!!!" my son sobbed. My daughter was crying. The dogs were scratching the door to be let out. *No more stories!*

Lesson #25: *Life isn't a fairy tale. And that's the bright side!*

PART V

UH, PRIORITIES ANYONE?

We're all trying to figure out what's *really* important. Maybe, intellectually, we know. We know, but we just can't convince the side of ourselves that suffers from low self-esteem, low self-worth, bad habits, self-centeredness, self-gratification, insecurity, skin rashes and lesions, upper-respiratory congestion, and inner-ear wax build up.

"Wow!" people will say, standing on a vista somewhere, looking out at an inspiring, breath-taking view of the world. *"This is what it's all about."* That's what they say. "Man, you just can't get any better than this." But then, in less than about three minutes flat, they'll be wondering why they can't take more vacations, why they don't get more time off, how they got stuck in such a pitiful job, why they don't get paid more, how much they want a new car, how they've been thinking about sex change operations . . .

"I wasn't invited to the party."

"Our house is too small."

"I can't believe that guy makes more money than I do."

"My kids are driving me crazy."

"I'm sick of bunions on my feet."

The truth is, it's hard to keep a healthy perspective. It's hard to understand priorities without periodically suffering through pain or hardship. The people who've just survived a flood, but have lost all their belongings, are not hugging each other gratefully and saying, *"Thank God we're alive—now if only the blasted gas prices would drop!"* or *"If people are going to drive so slowly, they ought to keep their fat butts on the right side of the goddamn road!"* or *"When my mother-in-law visits, she insists on doing the laundry! Can you believe that?!"*

Gosh, it's all so awful.

Which is why I've learned to turn down the static—ignore everything that isn't important, to focus on only those things that, in the Grand Scheme of Things, really matter. You know, like sleep. Being cool. Deciding to *not* make the bed. Deciding to whip my naked breasts out in public. Friends in high places. Access to a good plastic surgeon.

We can't control chaos. We can't change Idiots. So we have to learn how to be grateful for all of Life's infinite, uncontrollable, idiotic chaos.

The alternatives ain't that great.

26

Sleep—Your Top Priority

Through scientific measurement of the brain's electrical activity, it was discovered in the 1950s that there are two kinds of sleep: rapid-eye-movement (REM) sleep, and non-REM sleep (NREM).

In 1995, a third kind of sleep was discovered, known as (I'll Never) Get-Rest-Or-Understanding-With-Children-Career-or-Husbands, or more commonly, GROUCCH sleep.

Prior to this discovery, scientists had believed for years that there were only three states of consciousness—wakefulness, REM sleep, and NREM sleep.

Apparently none of those scientists has kids. Or dogs who bark at, say, air molecules, all night long. Or a spouse who forgets to turn the T.V. off. Or a job percolating with lathered-up stress.

Or all of the above.

And even with their full, uninterrupted nights of sleep, these lame-o scientists have been unable to figure out the biological function of GROUCCH sleep. For instance, while REM sleep is characterized by eye movements, irregular breathing and heart-rate, and NREM sleep is characterized by a decrease in brain activity, GROUCCH sleep seems to be in a category of its own.

During GROUCCH, muscle activity is high as the afflicted individual gets into and out of bed approximately *a million* times per night, often punctuating the activity with the sort of language normally associated with angry NFL coaches. There are rapid eye movements, but they are OPEN eye movements, as the individual wildly gropes around in the dark for, say, a pacifier. Or maybe, a pencil, to write down what he'll *really* tell his boss in the morning.

Breathing during GROUCCH is rapid and shallow, similar to that of a panting dog on a hot summer day, while the heart-rate is marked by frequent palpitations.

In addition, preliminary research often describes the daytime characteristics of the GROUCCH sleeper as "extremely agitated," "cranky," and suffering from an "apparent loss of memory."

"For women, perhaps GROUCCH sleep by night, and the resulting high agitation by day, help insure the safety of their offspring," one male researcher suggested at a recent conference at the University of Minnesota.

"Or maybe the highly agitated state is nature's way of providing future birth control," shot back a female colleague, while simultaneously dousing him with her Diet Coke, and stepping on his toes with her pumps.

Always ready to do my part for scientific research, I participated in early case studies on GROUCCH sleep, by providing information related to an experience at my bank one morning:

"May I have your social security number?" the bank teller asked.

"Can't remember it," I responded.

"Address? Phone number?"

"Oh, gee..."

"Well, I'm sorry but we can't—"

"OH YES YOU CAN. AND YOU'LL DO IT RIGHT NOW."

See? Memory loss! High agitation! The classic signs.

Other characteristics of GROUCCH sleepers include, but may not be limited to:

1. Lack of, or strangely applied, makeup;

2. Bird's nest hair;

3. Glazed-over, vacant look in the eyes;

4. Tendency to talk to themselves, or inanimate objects such as bananas, in the produce department; and

5. Mindless, incessant humming of "Barney" songs.

Although scientists theorize that "neurons" located in the brain stem may somehow be tied to the GROUCCH phenomenon, a GROUCCH sufferer, upon hearing this, reportedly said, "You can just shove your neurons, pal."

Lesson #26: *As you age, a number of hilarious things happen. For instance, your need for calories goes down, while your desire for dietary substances such as fat and alcohol go up. HA HA HA!*

Also, your need for sleep sharply increases, as the opportu-

nity for such sleep dramatically decreases.

Plan accordingly. Try to feel good enough about yourself that you're able to admit that, sure, family, friends, success, and finances are all well and fine, but that SLEEP, whenever or wherever you can get it, is the most important thing.

27

The Importance of Being Cool

Once when we were living in L.A., my husband wore his dark sunglasses inside a movie theatre. Was this cool? No. This was idiotic. He'd forgotten his regular glasses.

Not that coolness isn't important. It is. Particularly in terms of keeping perishable foods bacteria-free.

It's just that, coolness, as a function of attitude, is more complicated than mere refrigeration. Especially since, the harder you try to be cool, the more you're likely to look like a total loser.

For instance, I used to keep my car's windows rolled all the way down, even on cold, rainy days, so that people could hear me listening to the radio as I drove by. My hands would be beating rhythmically on the steering wheel, little Ms. Rhythm Doctor, even if it was only in time with the traffic and weather report.

I danced and moved and gyrated along with the beat of

that catchy traffic and weather report, and chewed gum with my mouth open. I thought I was being cool.

Someone once asked me, though, when I was stopped at a traffic light, break-dancing right there in the front seat, if there wasn't something wrong with my transmission. Was this a set-back for me? Well, yes. But then, it was a breakthrough of sorts. Because it dawned on me, then and there, that I had to get my priorities straight—I *had* to become cooler.

Being cool is hard to explain unless you know my husband. Then I'd say, being cool is everything OPPOSITE of him. For instance, you can't go to the hip, cool Spago's restaurant in L.A. and spend the entire dinner hour gawking. GOD! We had an anniversary dinner there, years ago, and nearly a divorce. Dork-o-Meister kept staring—*AND POINTING*—every time a familiar face walked in.

Another key part of being cool is being able to march confidently into a room and know, instinctively, just what to say. For years, I tried to heat things up at social gatherings by opening with the brilliant, if understated, *"Is it just me, or does it blow any of you people away that Archimedes' Principle maintains that buoyancy is the loss of weight an object seems to incur when it is placed in a liquid?"* This was totally ineffective. Apparently I'd grossly misjudged the general population's interest in physics. I also had very little luck with, *"Yikes, you know what? My arm-pits are itching something fierce."*

Forget what you've heard, originality is overrated.

So while others volunteered their time to charitable organizations, began recycling programs, and tried to make the world a better place, I got my priorities straight. I worked on being cool.

For instance, I learned that you can get most people's attention by walking into a room and stating, simply, *"I just shot a man."* That usually works. As does, *"Right now. I mean, right* now*! Does anyone want to have sex?"*

In addition to learning to say the right thing, I needed to work on a few coolness skills. For instance, during the summer time, it usually left the wrong impression as to how hip I really was when I didn't wash my hair or shave my legs for weeks on end. It also tended to send the wrong message when I squinted at wine lists for a really long time, finally requesting something that was really, really "fresh."

So I started eating arugula for breakfast, doggonit, bruschetta for lunch, and fresh fruit/goat cheese smoothies with wheat grass for that afternoon pick-me-up. I also learned the art of ordering a half-caf-half-decaf-extra-steam-hold-the-foam decaf.

Sure the public school system in our country needed improvement, sure voters were apathetic, sure folks needed job training. But I was becoming cool.

I even started leaving tips after dining in fine restaurants, and I stopped wearing athletic socks with skirts.

Lesson #27: *Cool has been, and will always be, important. As far back as 1861, for instance, the stylish Brits produced 83.6 million tons of cool! Likewise, those savvy, romantic French folks produced 6.8 tons of cool! And the Russians? With their tall, furry hats and vodka? They produced 300,000 tons of cool.*

Oh. Sorry. That was coal.

The point is, cool is better than coal, and it doesn't pollute.

28

Resolutions! Make Them! Keep Them!

I like to keep my promises. That's the kind of person I am. I have my priorities straight.

So after carefully reviewing years and years of failed New Year's resolutions—broken promises, if you will—I've decided that, no matter what, I'll KEEP my resolutions this year! I'll persevere! I will! And I'll do so, largely, by dramatically lowering my standards.

Therefore, I resolve to:

1. Not associate with any robber-barons from the late 19th and early 20th centuries, including both Vanderbilts and Rockefellers;

2. Not do any public speaking on the topics of: "Electroplating," "The Pros and Cons of DDT," "Electrolysis: Friend or Foe?" or "The Pythagorean Theorem: Did We Really Need to Spend So Much Blasted Time on It in School?" I will remain steadfast in this conviction, even if there are considerable speaking

fees and/or worthy charities involved;

3. *Not* injure or maim any fellow human beings for the following irritating behaviors: Foot-tapping in movies, knee-bouncing in movies, excessive need for restroom use in movies, excessive chewing of popcorn with an open mouth during quiet periods in movies, humming in movies or anywhere else;

4. Also, I will also try to avoid injuring or maiming the growing number of individuals who feel the need to take 45 MINUTES TO AN HOUR to properly add milk and various other accoutrements to their coffee at local coffee houses.

Further, I resolve to NOT:

5. Cross-dress in public;

6. Return videos on time;

7. Get call waiting;

8. Lose weight.

But, I will try to:

9. Limit the use of the word "dork" in all of my writing as requested by my agent, despite the truly astonishing number of "dork-like" individuals in all facets of my life, including, frequently, my agent;

10. Refrain from telling people who feel the need to always say, "I'm *soooo* busy!" to "get a catheter";

11. Refrain from telling people who feel the need to name drop to also "get a catheter" since, at the time of this writing, there is no medical evidence suggesting that this might benefit them.

At dinner parties, I resolve to:

12. Refrain from making any more pretentious references

to Plato, Aristotle, Goethe or Cervantes because, quite simply, my education does not allow for such references. I may, however, quote from Aeschylus and his complete works, trusting that no one will have the foggiest as to what, or whom, I'm speaking of. Including me.

Additionally, I will:

13. Make reference to "Whitman," commenting that "the guy really knows how to put together one helluva box of candy";

14. I will refrain from bringing an uninvited date, as this is considered rude and inappropriate behavior for a "happily married woman";

15. I will stop pronouncing the "*s*" in "hors d'oeuvre";

16. I will not ask my host if there's a choice of entrees, commenting that "over-cooked food is against my religion."

Finally, I resolve to:

17. Be late getting my son to school. I will rationalize this behavior by reminding myself that the lateness provided us additional quality time, and that, for God's sake, the kid will be in school for many years of his life. Furthermore, I will feel compelled to offer lame excuses and/or foolish grins by way of explanation to any teachers;

18. With increasing, if not disturbing regularity, use the following phrases with my kids and/or husband: "Okay, I'm NOT going to say it again," "Okay, if I HAVE to say it again . . ." and "Okay, by the TIME I count to three . . ."

Lesson #28: *Being a good person involves keeping your promises to both yourself and to others. The best way to do this*, of *course, is to lower your standards! Resolve to do it!*

29

Why Are You Making the Bed?

I'm important, my life is important, my time is important, my time matters. I've got my priorities clear.

In other words, I've stopped making the bed.

It wasn't easy. For years, I'd been an anal-retentive, compulsive bed-maker, fluffing the pillows, smoothing the blankety blank blanket. I was the sort of person who relished alphabetized rows of soup cans, and all other forms of order.

"My life is so disorganized and crazy!" I remember a friend telling me.

Oh yeah? Well we all make our beds and lie in them, I thought, smugly.

Clearly, I had to reach down deep within myself for the courage and strength to overcome this annoying bed-making foible. I suffered through turbulent days and fitful nights. I wept uncontrollably. I threw objects across rooms. My hands shook, and I perspired like Tom Jones in concert.

I looked for help.

There were no "Stop the Madness (of Bed-making)" support groups. There were no self-help books in the library entitled *The Courage to Go Un-Made*. There were no little patches to stick on my arm.

So, just like the time I had front row center seats for *Cats*, I had to bravely, painfully, gut it out.

It's sad, really, how far we all deviate from our roots. Could it have been so long ago that my mother's voice trilled in my ears, the monotonous refrain, "Make your bed! Make your bed!"

"I'm just going to mess it up again, though," I responded, quite cleverly, I thought.

"Right—and with *that* attitude, why would you ever take a bath, or clean up your room?" my mother asked.

"You bring up two excellent points," I agreed enthusiastically. "In fact, I don't want to take baths, or clean up my room, either."

Unfortunately, our household wasn't based on the tenets of democracy, so I was forced to not only take baths and clean my room, I had to make the bed.

Sure, it could have been worse. At least I *had* a bed. A bed free of vermin, that is, something which has always been a priority of mine since reading Leonardo da Vinci complain, in the 15th century, of having to spend the night "upon the spoils of dead creatures."

Mattresses, back then, were made of straw, leaves, and pine needles that mildewed, rotted, and became a popular hangout for rats, mice, and all their friends and relatives.

Fortunately, in the 1500's, the French came up with something called the "wind bed," which, I'm told, had nothing to do with flatulence. Rather, it was an air mattress made from heavily waxed canvas, which often cracked in the middle of the night.

The British first developed spring mattresses in the early 18th century. Interestingly, the springs often snapped, giving rise to what is known in the current day as acupuncture.

It wasn't until 1925 that the U.S. manufacturer Zalmon Simmons received tremendous attention for having a really weird name. Also, he produced the first "Beautyrest" innerspring mattress and launched a marketing campaign which has, in modern day, given rise to ads involving bowling balls.

All of this should tell you, dear reader, one important thing—that progress comes with a price. When we, as a civilization, went from sleeping on dead animals to spring mattresses, it meant that we had to get sheets, pillowcases, dust ruffles, and other annoying and color-coordinated linens. We were expected to make our beds look good!

Lesson #29: *You (haven't) made your bed, but you can still lie in it. Life, and the robust living of it, is simply too darn short for organization. Why focus all that time and energy on a pointless task like making your blasted bed, every day, when you could be doing more meaningful things, like watching "Wheel of Fortune?"*

30

Nutrition and Nudity

I admit it.

There was a time, before the birth of my first child, when I actually thought women should *not* whip out their naked breasts in public.

I'd pass these creepy, Earth-Mother Exhibitionists occasionally, desperately trying to calm some thrashing, squealing infant, hunkered over on a bench maybe, or in the corner of a restaurant, a blanket feebly draped over their little squirmer, trying, usually with little success, to be as discreet as possible.

And I'd actually see their naked bosom!

Ladies! *Ladies*! I'd think. For crying out loud, can't we sequester this sort of private, personal activity to the privacy of our homes?

Not that I have anything against breasts. Breasts are fine.

Without them, there'd be no *National Geographic*.

It's just that, like so many of us, I'd been conditioned to believe that they belonged in, well, Victoria's Secret catalogs. On models with pouty lips and come-hither expressions. And, quite frankly, the phrase "impressive bust" did not conjure up visions of law enforcement activity.

When I got pregnant, my husband and I enrolled in a breast-feeding class where we learned that, despite his sensitive and supportive nature, he was not qualified for the task.

Again, we were subjected to the sight of many naked breasts. Healthy breasts, unhealthy breasts, breasts at work, breasts on vacation, breasts on parade.

The class discussions made me cringe.

"Nipple, nipple . . . blah, blah . . . nipple . . . nipple," our instructor said.

"Nipple . . . blah . . . nipple?" someone asked.

"Good nipple question," she answered. "Nipple . . . blah, blah . . . nipple."

Yikes!

Two babies later, I hardly bother to wear clean clothes, wash my hair, find matching socks. About as far from a Victoria's Secret model as, say, a Ford Explorer. And I often find myself promenading around the grocery store, the office, the town, ready, at any moment, to feed my hungry infant.

"You breast-feed in *public*?!" my childless friend Wendy asked with such horror that you'd have thought that I'd just said "pee" in public. "I can't believe it—*YOU*, of all people, breast-feed in public?"

"NO! God, no!" I said. "Only if the baby is hungry.

Because the truth of the matter is, I'm now a living, breathing, lactating, mammalian manufacturer, producer, and distributor of a high-quality dairy product. I'm so excited about this role, in fact, that I'm thinking about branching off into ice cream and cottage cheese.

I'm a mom. Which means that my life is a complicated, chaotic, frenzied jumble, both wonderful and trying, exhilarating and exhausting. It means that I never get to go to the bathroom by myself.

And it means feeding my little one at the exact moment when her little tummy grumbles. When it comes to public nudity, then, as a mom, at least I have my priorities right.

Lesson #30: *Someone once said, "Do not judge, and you will not be judged. Do not condemn, and you will not be condemned." Which isn't to say that if you see someone on the street with pierced eyebrows that this chap is normal. Certainly, in some circumstances, you should feel free to judge, judge, judge. All you want. And the guy with the weird hair? Judge him, too.*

Just make it a priority to be there for your kids when they need you.

31

The Truth Is the Ticket

I once took a very bad fall off a horse and, since I was speaking a language currently unknown on this planet, and not getting up, an ambulance took me to the hospital emergency room. Riding along in that ambulance, I was nervous, in pain, and breathing with difficulty.

In other words, it was exactly like the feeling I experienced recently, when I was driving along and a state trooper appeared in my rear view mirror, lights flashing.

Talk about an immediate physiological response!

I was panting, having heart palpitations, trying to maintain sphincter control, and sweating like Albert Brooks in *Broadcast News*.

"Why didn't you try to talk your way out of the ticket?" a friend later asked me.

That's rich. I'd rather sit through sixteen performances of the local high school's performance of *Oklahoma!* than try to get creative with a police officer.

I can remember the first time I was ever pulled over. I'd just gotten my license and was going 5 mph over the speed limit. Okay, maybe it was 25. I was horrified. I had actually *broken the law* — I was like *a fugitive* or something — and I was *getting busted*.

The experience was nearly as humiliating as the time back in kindergarten when I was performing in a ballet recital to a song called "Jack in the Box."

The dance opened with three of us ballerinas jumping out of our boxes — except that Mary Jo Biker, a young girl of remarkable girth, didn't quite clear the side of her box, and there was a sound on that stage not unlike a stampeding herd of African elephants.

On both occasions — getting pulled over by a police officer and trying to leap and plié — while an entire audience was buckled over busting their guts laughing — my brain turned into tapioca.

I went blank.

Vacated the premises.

Checked into the Mindless Mute Motel.

The point is: I am physically and emotionally incapable of talking my way out of a traffic ticket.

Oh sure, I know people who do it. Who come up with *contrived*, *elaborate*, and *far-fetched* stories. And certainly, one would think that coming up with *contrived*, *elaborate*, and *far-fetched* stories would be right up my alley.

But no.

"Maybe you're just intimidated by authority figures," a friend suggested.

You mean, just because I once had a conversation with a doctor that went something like this:

Lindsey: How are you?

Doctor: Fine. How are you?

Lindsey: Fine. How are you?

Doctor: Uh . . . what're you here for today?

Lindsey: Fine. How are you?

A good friend of mine, a police officer, had another suggestion—but it was too crazy and unrealistic to consider, namely, *not* speeding.

"Don't you have any *useful* suggestions?" I responded.

"Yeah—at least say something to the officer. You never know."

With that, I bought a book, written by a highway patrolman, that provided documented, *on-file* examples of excuses people have tried:

"The telephone pole was approaching fast. I was attempting to swerve out of its path when it struck my front end."

"I was on my way to the doctor's with rear end trouble when my universal joint gave way causing me to have an accident."

"The truck carelessly backed through my windshield into my wife's face."

"The pedestrian had no idea what direction to go, so I ran over him."

Lesson #31: *"That's not a lie," Alexander Haig once said, "It's a terminological inexactitude." Get your priorities straight. If you can't tell the truth, or at least make up something interesting, then don't say anything at all.*

PART VI

THE WORLD IS FULL OF IDIOTS

"In the first place," Mark Twain once wrote, "God made idiots. This was for practice. Then He made School Boards."

And after that, homeowners' associations, review committees, politicians, government officials, bureaucrats, inept bosses, annoying relatives, in-laws, back-stabbing co-workers, petty and jealous friends, conniving car salespeople, shock jocks, telephone solicitors, bill collectors, know-it-alls, backseat drivers, Monday morning quarterbacks, David Hasselhoff, Tori Spelling, the DMV, fitness fanatics, elitist snobs, and pseudo-intellectuals.

"To be ignorant of one's ignorance is the malady of the ignorant," wrote Amos Alcott. I wish I knew what that means, but I'm too ignorant.

Basically, though, I think it means that the world is full of idiots.

Years ago, my first published story appeared on the front page of one of the sections in the *Los Angeles Times*. Front and center. It was a light-hearted, amusing little banter about dinner parties. I joked playfully about the fun of sitting next to someone you didn't like, who talked about something you weren't interested in, while you ate food you hadn't ordered. HA HA HA HA. I did not ONCE mention abortion, prayer in schools, gun regulation, or the death penalty. AND I GOT A RECORD AMOUNT OF OUTRAGED MAIL!

"Who do you think you are?!" one angry writer demanded. "My husband and I love having barbecues, we make our own sauce, and everyone eats corn on the cob and this great dessert I make with Cool Whip! I hope you get RUN OVER BY A BUS!"

"Dear Lindsey," another reader wrote, "HOW DARE YOU!! I'll bet you're an elitist snob who only goes out to the most expensive, trendy restaurants! I'll bet you like public radio!! You're the kind of person who gives L.A. a bad name."

Whoa. That one hurt. Particularly since, at the time, I was so sub-poor that my dining-out experiences were limited to the sorts of restaurants that served ketchup in little plastic packets.

The truth is, there is a lot that's funny about dinner parties. There's a lot that's funny about just about everything in life—relationships, family, work, recreation, hobbies—if you look for it. What's great about living is that we get to make choices. We can lighten up about everything, stop taking it all so seriously, and bring our blood pressure down.

Or we can just be idiots.

32

Idiots Behind Wheels

Excuse me, but what's this business about cars flashing their headlights at you because they're annoyed? Like what, you're driving along, and someone flashes his lights at you, and so you immediately, shamefully, pull off the road to evaluate your driving skills?

Personally, it's given my entire driving experience a perpetual strobe effect.

And what's this business about annoyed drivers pulling up next to you in order to make a really nasty face, before proceeding past you? That made me so mad the last time someone did that, I raced right back up to his rear bumper, and started flashing my lights. THAT'LL SHOW HIM!

My mom's driving annoys me; there's so much tension and high drama. "*Oh, GOD, I almost missed that exit!*" she'll shriek, gripping the wheel nervously, frantically checking the rear view mirror, the exit still approximately three miles ahead. "God, I wonder if I'm going to be able to get in the right lane?!" Well, gee. Maybe. Considering we're already *in* the right lane.

Likewise, my dad ought to be a missionary. People riding in the car with him, when he's driving, tend to get religious. "Oh God!" they scream. "Oh God! Oh God!"

He tailgates. He tailgates with a capitol "T" that rhymes with "D" that stands for Death, Death, Death, Death.

He tailgates in such a convincing manner that passengers forget all about the petty worries in their lives—the office politics, the leaking faucet, the impending triple-bypass surgery—and focus on what's really important, namely, updating their life insurance policies and planning a way to escape the vehicle alive.

And unlike many drivers who tend to be destination-oriented, my dad's purpose behind the wheel seems to involve riding up on automobiles' rear bumpers, perversely uttering "Crunch," and then topping off the whole buffoonery with a verbal assault.

"Stupid Maryland drivers!" he snaps at drivers of cars with Maryland plates. "Stupid Virginia drivers!" he says in such a way that you'd rather be shot than be accused of being a Virginia driver. "Stupid Washington, D.C., drivers!"

Maybe it's genetic. My sister Leigh isn't such a hot driver either. In fact, she drives so fast that the skin on passengers' cheeks flaps around like they're in a NASA training module, the G-force taking its toll.

And she's the only person I know who, on a busy Saturday night, pulled a U-turn in Georgetown, the hopping, trendy nightclub and restaurant section of Washington, D.C., that's packed with cars and pedestrians. She was going so fast I thought the car was going to tilt up on one side, like some Evel Knievel driving stunt, and all her passengers went slamming over to one side of the car. She quietly prefaced this bladder-control-losing maneuver with a simple, although in retrospect somewhat manic statement: "Here we go."

Determined to not let idiot drivers intimidate me, I decided to face my fears and frustrations. I married one. He's a great guy, sure. But behind the wheel, my husband is easily distracted. For instance, probing questions such as, "How was your day?" are enough to have him careening up onto the sidewalk.

Plus, he has this little problem of steering *toward* whatever he happens to be looking at, so if we're driving through a nice neighborhood and he spots a pretty home, there's a half-decent chance we're going to ram into someone's curb.

Worse yet, a friend of mine can never leave well enough alone. A "surge-and-jam" driver, she's always in the process of actively accelerating, or actively braking.

The accelerations tend to be violent "surges," whipping passengers' heads back against the headrests. The braking is nothing short of shocking, "jamming" the passengers' heads and bodies forward. If someone were to film the car driving by, it'd look like the passengers were wildly dancing to some heavy metal tune.

Sometimes, I wish that any of these drivers would encounter my brother-in-law out on the road. As CEO of the cuss-and-go school—a driving method that consists of 5 percent actual driving and 95 percent foul-mouth expletives used in remarkable new and unusual patterns—he'd have a field day behind another friend of mine at a red light.

She happens to be one of those loads who just sits there, oblivious, when the light turns green, happily using that red-light down-time to look for receipts in her purse, neaten up the car, file her nails.

People behind her tend to get so infuriated that they immediately convert to the cuss-and-go method on the spot.

Fortunately, now there's help for all of them.

There's group therapy. Seriously.

In Massachusetts, motorists who cause five accidents, or get five or more moving violations within three years, must attend eight hours of "reality therapy," during which the offenders sit around in groups of up to twenty and talk about all their complicated, psychosomatic motivations for driving the way they do.

I told my dad about it one day as he was riding up on someone's fender.

"I could save them—*crunch*—a lot of—*crunch*—time and money in therapy," he said. "Because, basically, they're all just stupid Massachusetts drivers!"

Lesson #32: *"A car can massage organs which no masseur can reach," French author Jean Cocteau tells us. "It is the one remedy for the disorders of the great sympathetic nervous system. The craving for opium can be endured in the car."*

Mother of God! Is that creepy, or what? This guy was out on the roads?! Doing his drug rehab therapy?!

Life is not a line-drive. It's not a simple shot from point A to point B. There are risks. It can be scary. And sometimes you'll be driven to distraction.

But don't let the idiots drive you crazy.

33

Insincere Idiots

I recently received a thank-you note for a wedding present that said: *"Thank you ever so much for the wonderful gift. It was very thoughtful of you and a very wonderful gift. We will think of you whenever we look at the gift."*

Whoa. Talk about heart-felt. Talk about personal.

Not that I write the most articulate and poetic thank-you notes—in fact, I can't remember the last time I even wrote a thank-you note. But if I did, I assure you, I would never have written this line:

"Thank you for the high-speed, electric can-opener designed for under the cabinet use, in its designer color, with its three-year warranty."

I mean really, is it so hard? Is it so hard to be grateful, personal, and sincere, while simultaneously engaging a writing style at the third-grade level or above?

I'd rather get something—*anything*—more inspired.

"The other day a rank, nauseatingly foul odor blasted my brains out as I was opening a can of my dog's Alpo with that lame-o gift you sent. I dry-heaved, broke a sweat, then thought of you. Thanks for such a special gift."

Or:

"To be honest, I have always wondered what has happened in a person's life, what horrible disappointments and abuse a person has endured, that he or she would be moved to actually purchase, as a gift, a can-opener. On the up side, it has greatly expedited the process of making tuna."

Hey, I'm not out in left field on this one—even Emily Post, the empress of etiquette, says that the "most important qualifications of a thank-you letter are that it sounds sincere and that it be written promptly."

Except that "promptly" is a relative term, which I tend to loosely define as "sometime before death." Because, for the love of Hallmark, don't we all have better things to do besides write prompt thank-you notes?

The key, then, is to be sincere. Or, at least, to come off as sincere, even if that means being a little creative. Or lying.

As when my husband and I once received a pair of His and Hers bath towels. It's a real luxury to have a plush bath towel with a name embroidered on it, particularly when—and maybe I'm being picky here—it's *your* name.

My towel had "Mary Beth" written on it. A fine name, certainly. Just not mine. What should I have done? Written a thank you note signed "Mary Beth"? Written a note on personalized stationery with my name underlined?

Instead, I sent a thank-you note to the gift giver, Elaine, which said:

Dear Ginger,

Towels! Towels! Everyone can always use towels. Especially when they're wet! Now all I have to do is have someone over named Mary Beth. Or buy a dog! Ha Ha! You're wonderful, you're such a kidder. Don't ever change.

Signed, Lindsey.

I hope you've learned something from all this.

Also, I really want to thank you for taking the time to buy my book. It was very wonderful of you to spend some hard-earned cash on my little literary endeavor. I mean, to go to the bookstore and stuff like that. And then, you know, like, to read it. Once again, I'd like to say that I really appreciate how wonderful you were to take the time to buy my book. Using your own money and all. And reading it.

Sincerely yours,

Lindsey

Lesson #33: *Tennessee Williams said: "Everyone says he's sincere, but everyone isn't sincere. If everyone was sincere who says he's sincere there wouldn't be half so many insincere ones in the world and there would be lots, lots, lots more really sincere ones!"*

Okay . . . you don't have to be THAT sincere.

34

Shake Hands with an Idiot

Carp. Mackerel. Flounder. This is what I was thinking about when, recently, I was introduced to someone, and then we shook hands.

It was a cold, clammy, halibut-like sort of handshake, and afterward I glanced down at my hand, checking for scales. No, there were no scales, but right off, I knew this person had serious problems.

The point is, forget about what kinds of cars people drive, how they dress, or where they live. Forget about whether they butter their bread or dip it in olive oil, whether they like foreign movies with subtitles or American ones. Because whether it's Capitol Hill or Beverly Hills, you can tell a lot about what kind of idiot a person is by how he or she shakes your hand.

Which, by the way, you positively don't do in Beverly Hills. Instead, you offer fake little, non-touching kisses on either side of the person's face, like you were brought up in Europe, when in fact you weren't, and then you follow the ghastly gesture with the statement, "I'll call you."

I remember my first greeting exchange gone awry in Beverly Hills. I was about to greet an acquaintance of mine, but didn't know that she was coming in for the fake-kissing thing, as I was simultaneously initiating a handshake.

The result? I slugged her so hard in the stomach with my innocently outstretched hand that, for several moments, she stood there doubled over gasping and speaking in tongues. I heard, later, that after this tragic incident, her personal trainer decided to focus more daily attention on firming her abs.

Hey, I was only "reaching out enthusiastically," as my dad used to instruct us. *"When you're greeting someone, always extend your hand enthusiastically, grasp their hand firmly, and look them straight in the eyes. Show some class."* Unfortunately, this little directive gave my brother license to regularly crush the bones of his sisters' hands into sand for many years to come, initiating a spirited exchange which often included, but was not limited to, saturating his pillowcase with antiperspirant.

Adult bone-crushers, I've found, tend to be businesspeople who are not doing all that well, so they compensate with a pulverizing death-grip. "It's great to see you!" they say with false levity, destroying the bone structure in your hand. Idiots.

The other mutilating idiots work on Capitol Hill.

I've worked on Capitol Hill, so I know. Success there is measured by: (a) the ability to sound like you know what you're talking about, when you almost never do—or maybe that was just me; and (b) the ability to make mincemeat of others' hands.

The "power" handshake probably has its origins in folklore. Long ago, when a villager met a man he didn't recognize, he reacted by automatically reaching for his dagger. The stranger did likewise, and the two cautiously circled each other until they became satisfied that the situation was safe, or until a major playoff game was coming on the TV. Then, daggers were reinserted into their sheaths, and right hands were extended in goodwill.

And since women, throughout history, weren't the bearers of weapons, unless you count PMS, they never fully developed the custom of the handshake.

Instead, women often practice a little hand maneuver that involves grasping the fingertips of the person whom they are greeting, as if full-hand contact is going to give them herpes.

I HATE that squirrelly finger-tip thing. It's weird. Not as weird, perhaps, as the fact that there's an exhibit called "Flight Time Barbie," as in Barbie doll, at the Smithsonian's National Air and Space Museum in Washington, D.C., an exhibit that uses dolls to show the progress of women in flight and space exploration careers. But still, weird.

The only thing worse than the power-handshake and the finger-pinch—not including the PBS children's television show "Teletubbies," with its clever storylines that involve Teletubby characters repeatedly falling over—is when someone grabs your hand with *two* hands. And they keep holding on! Until your mutual hand sweat is abundant enough to raise the ocean's water level by several inches. Because compared to that, I'd rather get a handshake more along the lines of cold, poached salmon.

Lesson #34: *As far as personalities go, a handshake can really show one's hand.*

35

Bureaucracy Is Idiotic

"Common sense," Voltaire said, "is not so common."

Idiocy, in fact, is more common, as is conformity. Which is why I wish my writing career involved concocting the written portion of the Department of Motor Vehicles (DMV) driving exam.

Primary qualification for the job? You have to be an idiot. Can you imagine? The competition for those jobs must be fierce. Not that I haven't been surrounded by bureaucratic stupidity before. Remember? I've worked in the federal government. It's frustrating! It's annoying! The upside? It can also be pretty entertaining.

Here's a question from my driver's exam:

(1) If you become sleepy while driving, it is best to:

    (a) Increase your speed to get away from other vehicles;

    (b) Drink coffee to make you more alert;

(c) Play the radio loudly; or

(d) Drive to a safe place, stop, and rest.

The correct answer is (d)! Seriously. And I can certainly understand why. Why, there's nowhere I'd rather close my eyes, let my guard down, and have a nice relaxing rest than alongside the great highways of North America. Come to think of it, why ever bother with a hotel? In a car, you can conveniently leave all your money and valuables right out there on the seat next to you!

"Uh, excuse me," I said to the inanimate Test-Correcting Man. "Shouldn't the answer be: 'Drink coffee, play the radio loudly, drive with your head out the window, think about visiting your in-laws, and periodically slap yourself silly'?"

I could tell he really liked my answer, my special little spark, by the way he remained perfectly motionless without ONCE blinking his eyes. Next question:

(2) Should you often check traffic behind you?

(a) Yes, but only if you are slowing down;

(b) Yes, you will know if you are being followed by a tailgater;

(c) No, you should pay attention to the vehicles in front of you; and

(d) Only if there is a really hot member of the opposite sex behind you.

Okay, I missed that question, too—the DMV'ers aren't big on write-in responses. The correct answer is (b).

"'B?' You're kidding, right?" I said to Non-Blinking Man. "You're joshing me."

"Driving manual," he grumbled, his lips unmoving.

"My point is that it's a broad, misleading question, and there are all sorts of times when you should *NOT* be checking the rear-view mirror," I said. "Say there was, like, a gang murder going on in front of me. Later, the police would ask me for details. I'd say, 'Gee, officers, I don't know how tall they were or what color shirts they were wearing, I was too busy checking my rear-view mirror for tailgaters.' "

"And say there was, oh, a meteor shower right in front of me, or a small aircraft attempting an emergency landing on the freeway. The headlines would have fun with that—'*Pilot Lands Safely on Freeway, Run Over by Woman Checking Her Rear-View Mirror.*' "

Little beads of embalming fluid were starting to appear on his forehead. Perhaps someone was at home.

(3) You have a condition on your license that states, "May drive from sunrise to sunset." It is 9:30 p.m. and you want to go to the store for cough medicine. What should you do?

"Listen," I said to Mr. Ready-to-Revoke. "This is getting just plain *goofy*! I *don't* have a condition on my license addressing sunrise and sunset, nor do I need cough medicine. So the question—and I mean this in the nicest way possible—is on heroin. Totally irrelevant. Not applicable."

"Miss one more and that's it," he said jovially.

(4) Using the unpaved shoulder of the road to pass on the right side of the vehicle ahead of you is:

　　(a) Permitted if there are two or more lanes traveling in your direction;

　　(b) Not permitted;

　　(c) Permitted if you are turning right; or

　　(d) Permitted if the vehicle ahead is turning left.

"Look, I don't want to get existential on you, but these answers are a little too black and white. The real world just isn't that neat and tidy," I said. "I mean, what if *Godzilla* is blocking all the traffic lanes? Or a stampede of animals like in the movie *Jumanji* comes by, and your friend is about to deliver a baby in the back seat of the car? My friend, *look out*, I'm going out on the shoulder!"

Eventually, because I'd been there the better part of the day, I compromised my principles and gave them the answers I knew they were looking for. It was an exhausting, undignified experience, and I'd been beaten by a bunch of idiots.

Lesson #35: *Eugene McCarthy said at least one true thing: "The thing that saves us from the bureaucracy is inefficiency. An efficient bureaucracy is the greatest threat to liberty." The up-side? Bureaucratic stupidity, while frightening, can be pretty entertaining.*

36

Health Club Idiots

"5, 6, 7, 8 . . . " The sound was coming from the "fitness room."

"*. . . two more times, one more time . . .*"

I was at the health club. For the first time in two years. Okay, four years. And, apparently, things had changed. And I'm not just talking about the width of my butt. I opened the door and was greeted by the Radio City Rockettes.

Where were all the sweating, grunting, sweat-shirt clad people? The push-ups, the jumping jacks?

"*Feel the burn, feel the burn,*" Joan Lunden sang out, chirpily, from the front of the room. Women with coiffed hair, perfect makeup and nails, clad in the sort of leotards one might suspect to encourage any number of infections, felt the burn. They flexed and gyrated. They skipped and hopped. Strange thing was, I couldn't help noticing, these babes were all ready in shape! What, for the love of God, were they doing here?! Idiots!

And then there was me. Standing in the doorway like Woody Allen entering an NFL locker room, standing in the doorway in my baggy gray sweat pants and t-shirt.

Bouffants turned. Hmmm. I considered saying that I was the janitor. That I'd be back later. To do the floors.

But I'd resolved to start an exercise program, to tone, strengthen, and stretch, so I found a space in the back.

"Let's take it from the top!" Perky One chirped with the same kind of enthusiasm I might reserve for, say, spotting a Dairy Queen in an unfamiliar town.

". . . up and down, and inhale . . . and exhale. . . ."

Fitness.

Health clubs.

Perfect hair, nails, and make up.

Please.

Yeah, I know that working out regularly is supposed to increase energy, bone strength, cardiovascular endurance, lung capacity, circulation and metabolism, typing speed and accuracy, reading comprehension, and the ability to floss teeth in fifteen seconds or less.

I've read that regular exercise is supposed to increase creativity and raise sexual interest, although the article did not clarify *whose*. I know all that.

But the coordinated outfits? The trendy exercise apparatus? The lack of *actual sweating*? What's that all about?!

Clearly, though, I needed help.

I'd tried to exercise in my home, but was unsuccessful due to the competing nature of readily available chocolate products.

I tried running. Forget running. People who run are idiots, and I mean that in the nicest way possible. I'd get so bored running that at times I actually considered hurling myself into oncoming traffic just to break the monotony.

I tried golfing, which I enjoyed—not only for its lack of actual physical activity, but also because, by comparison to a lot of the men out there, I felt like a young, well-dressed, svelte woman. It's just that I wasn't getting any actual exercise.

I even tried swimming. I figured I could get up every morning and swim a few laps in our backyard pool. It sounded doable. Until it dawned on me that we didn't have a backyard pool.

So I joined a health club.

I paid money to see women who really shouldn't run around the locker room—*naked*.

I paid money to step on and off a little "step" platform in time to disco hits of the '70s.

I paid money to look like a sorry, stupid idiot in the weight room when I'd use the Nautilus equipment incorrectly. For instance, a low, flat area looked like a good place to stretch out and rest. Turns out it moves like a conveyor belt. You're supposed to walk on it.

Eventually, I realized that I had paid money to learn three key things about fitness: you can't exercise unless you already look good; you can't exercise without a little white towel draped around your neck at all times; and you don't show up at the club without an Evian bottle in tow.

Lesson #36: *"Almost every man wastes part of his life,"* Samuel Johnson once said, *"in attempts to display qualities which he does not possess." In a perfect world, it just wouldn't matter what we looked like. We'd be comfortable with ourselves.*

It isn't a perfect world, though. Appearances matter. Which is why folks really ought to stop wearing those crotchy leotards and ridiculous leg-warmers out in public.

37

Sometimes I'm an Idiot

In the category of "Finding New and Exciting Ways to Make a Complete Fool of Myself," I recently recorded my first story for public radio. I was, in short, an idiot. And by "idiot," I mean A TOTAL MORON. Incoherent. Uncomfortable with English as a language. Knocking things over that were not designed to be knocked over.

The bright side? All the sweat loss flushed the toxins out of my skin. Besides, sometimes we all look like idiots.

The purpose of the broadcasting stint was not so much to entertain and amuse radio audiences across the country, as it turned out. Rather, it was to: (a) See if I could grind my molars into a fine, dust-like powder; and (b) See how many times I could stumble over certain extremely-difficult-to-pronounce-words such as "the" and "so" and the always-tricky "and."

This isn't the first time I've been an idiot in public.

There was the skiing incident many years ago when, attempting to execute a stylish and athletic stop at the bottom of a ski run, in front of a very handsome man with a chiseled chin, I plowed into him.

And I mean "plowed" in its purest agrarian sense: I knocked that bad boy over and *planted* him into the earth. And due to the rarely-seen-in-such-panoramic-scope Domino Effect of Ski Lines, before it was over, the whole area had been flattened.

Then there was the time I went boating with some urbane people wearing Ralph Lauren sweaters. Dressed in new white pants and my cheap, knock-off nautical sweater, I took a misstep, slipped, hit the table, and had a major nosebleed over much of the catered lunch.

The point, therefore, is that this radio thing shouldn't have thrown me. Even when Steve, the producer of the show, said, "I don't mean to be rude, or anything, but what's the deal with your voice?" He may have been referring to the fact that I sounded like Alvin, of Alvin and the Chipmunks.

"I'm nervous."

Steve tried to put me at ease, then, by demystifying some of the highly technical—and intimidating—recording studio equipment.

"What's this?" I asked, pointing at a rather large piece of wooden equipment.

"A chair," he said.

Ahhh.

"And this?" I asked.

"Lysol brand disinfectant," he said. "Everyone around here has colds."

Fascinating.

"And this?"

"Water. In a paper cup. You drink it."

Man. *Unreal.*

"Can you imagine how all this modern-day technology would have blown away Lee De Forest, back in 1906?" I asked Steve, who was busy turning dials and flipping switches in an effort to get my voice to sound less rodent-y.

Lee De Forest, by the way, built the first amplifying vacuumtube, hooked it up to a wireless telegraph, and—*boom*— a few years later we had Howard Stern attempting to make his private parts a topic for household conversation.

Of course, back then few people owned radio receivers, so broadcasts mostly entertained nautical radio operators—folks who you'd expect to be avid radio fans since the alternative choice for fun was scrubbing the decks.

And then, by the end of 1921, eight commercial stations were providing news commentary and music over the American airwaves. By the mid-1930s, almost every American household had a radio.

Which is exactly what I was thinking about—how many people own radios—when someone finally told me to "relax."

Relax?

Oh, right. I get goofy, self-conscious and red-faced just recording messages for my own answering machines, sometimes spending the better part of a weekend repeating, over and over, "Hello, you've reached . . . " sounding more forced and moronic each time.

Then again, nothing ventured, nothing gained. Sometimes being an idiot is the price to pay for moving to the next level. So I took a deep breath, knocked my entire cup of water down the front of my shirt, and recorded the blasted story.

Later when I heard the recording, I had to really smile and congratulate myself for walking into a new and scary situation, even though I sounded like some sort of freak in desperate need of throat and larynx surgery, not to mention powerful tranquilizers.

Lesson #37: *Go ahead, take a deep breath, look like an idiot. Hey, sound like an idiot. Dare to be an idiot. Sometimes idiocy is the price we pay for moving into unchartered waters, climbing to the next level. It can be liberating. But not always.*

A FINAL WORD

While driving down a New Jersey highway one night, Paul and his wife, Bonnie—true story—decided to do what so many of us do when driving down highways late at night. They lit a stick of dynamite and tossed it out of their car.

Except that, *oops*, they'd forgotten to roll down the window. I hate it when that happens. Paul ended up in the hospital, Bonnie was charged with drunk driving.

I'm grateful for so many things in my life—the birds, the trees, early morning dew, credit cards with airline travel miles, alpha-hydroxy formulas—and for the fact that I don't have to take any long driving vacations with that fun couple.

But think about it. When we stop and think about all the blessings in our lives, it turns out that there are more than we can count. It's just that we usually don't think about them until something really bad happens.

And bad things do happen. Life takes unexpected turns, and there are certain elements we simply cannot control. Which is why I have such a hard time understanding why most people don't take better control of the parts of life that they can actually influence.

"God, I'm so tired."

"I'm exhausted, I was up with the kids three times last night."

"I'm sick of work."

"My husband never . . . "

"I was so mad that I had to stand in line for twenty minutes."

"The house is a mess."

"I wish I could afford a new car."

"I hate Mondays."

Pardon my gross oversimplification, folks, but perhaps we should be working to put things in perspective.

"Tell me three things you're grateful for, Jack," I said to my son from the kitchen one night as he sat watching a Pooh video. He didn't say anything for a long time. I thought he was contemplating the matter. Turned out he was watching Christopher Robin.

"JACK!"

"Huh?"

"Tell me three things you're grateful for," I repeated.

"Well . . . I like this video."

"What else?"

"I like treats, like cake."

"What else?"

"Jelly beans."

Hmmm. This was a little less cerebral, a little less philosophical than I had hoped for. "How about something other than treats, honey. What else makes you happy?"

"Everything, mommy. Except when I get ow-ies."

Unfortunately, life is full of ow-ies. And pain. And adversity. It can be frustrating! Disappointing! Infuriating! Empty! Overwhelmingly exhausting! And most of us have gotten really good at focusing, listing, and complaining about all the problems, the challenges, the static, then broadcasting it all, and putting it into syndication.

If we're going to keep score of all the bad stuff, why don't we keep score of the good things, too?

For instance, you never hear anyone say, "Gee, I'm having a really good day—my dental floss didn't rip behind my molars this morning, I don't have any red and oozing canker sores, I didn't get carjacked, mugged, or hit broadside on my way to work. Moreover, I haven't been summoned or sued, I'm not constipated, bloated, involved in any paternity cases, nor do I have conjunctivitis or inflamed and contagious rashes."

Well, thank God. No need to get *psycho* about it.

But still.

Why do we even bother to carry on sometimes? Why are we even here? Well, according to Barry Manilow, "We're all here for the same reason: to love me."

Smarmy crooners from the seventies notwithstanding, there's something else worth living for.

There are blessings.

It's a cliché to say, "Count your blessings," because the truth is, most of us, on some detached, intellectual level, know that we have an incredible number of wonderful blessings in our lives. It's just that somehow these blessings don't seem to have much impact on the day-to-day quality of our lives. Most people spend too much time worrying about all the wrong things.

"It takes all kinds, Linds."

Ignore what others may say or do. Focus on a few simple lessons. Learn to laugh. Embrace life's challenges. Alter expectations. Look on the bright side. Keep priorities straight.

And, above all, remember that we live on Planet Idiot.

Incredibly Useful Index

About the Author

Lindsey Stokes has worked in the U.S. Senate, the U.S. State Department, and several cheap chain restaurants. Currently, she lives in northern California with her husband, two children, three dogs, a horse, and a disturbing number of ants.

Her award-winning column appears in more than 120 newspapers nationwide. *Planet Idiot* is Lindsey's first book.